SELF-DISCOVERY QUESTIONS

Find Yourself and Your Life's Path in 5 Minutes a Day

GERALD CONFIENZA

Table of Contents

A Gift for You!

Most of the material I write about is centered on developing our inner selves. Thus, as you might've guessed, my readers are usually introverts. I can appreciate that because I'm an introvert myself. However, as an introvert, I'm also aware of our social shortcomings. Therefore, I've decided to gift you with some amazing material for your growth. By simply clicking the link below, you will have access to the *Introvert Survival Kit* and my *exclusive newsletter.*

Visit the following site or click here for full access:
http://bit.ly/introvertsk

This powerful bundle will help you make massive improvements in your social life. It contains 3 Ebooks and 2 articles:
- **EBook 1:** Making and Keeping Friends: Developing Friendships that Last a Lifetime in this Fast Paced World!
- **EBook 2:** How to Stop Worrying and Start Living Effectively In the 21st Century.
- **EBook 3:** High Impact Communication
- **And 2 Bonus Articles!**

Along with the material, you will also get a lot of value over the next few days. I'd recommend not missing out! Just go to
http://bit.ly/introvertsk

I also have a special invitation for those appreciate a good read...
If you'd like to be part of the review process of many of our upcoming books (and receive free copies!) and click here:
http://bit.ly/itadvancedreview I will send you details of what it entails through mail. Thanks!

Self-Discovery Journal:

200 Questions to Find Who You Are and What You Want in All Areas of Life

Introduction

"The unexamined life is not worth living."

- *Plato*

What would happen if you had a child and left him or her unattended without care or attention for a day?

How about a couple of weeks? Even worse, how about several months or years?

I know, it's almost too cruel to think about.

This book is written to bring awareness to the child we've left unattended for far too long- the one that lives inside of every one of us. As kids, we're in full connection with this child. We run, we play, we chase after things that we enjoy and love. We may not realize it, but we're deeply connected to who we are and what we want. We need not label ourselves to know who we are, or question why it is we want things; our present-moment living grants us a tacit answer to these questions. I would even venture to say that this is the main reason why childhood is so blissful for all of us.

As we grow older, we are introduced to words; and words have narrow meanings. Time and time again we've been labeled by our peers and parents through the use of these words. It's no wonder we lose most of our spontaneity as we mature; we've been identified by labels and we act as if we're programmed to follow them. In short, we lose sight of who we really are and what we really want. The recent onslaughts of existential crisis people across different age groups face only serve to prove this point.

Inside of us, there is a unique essence that seeks expression and individuality in all the things we do in the outside world. This may be but is not limited to our work life, family life, our spiritual life, our relationships, etc. However, until we are released from past conditioning, false beliefs of who we are, and repeating karmic cycles, our true essence will always remain imprisoned within us.

This is not the typical self-discovery journal. Most self-discovery journals delve straight into questions without first addressing the three points mentioned above. It's like trying to find a treasured item in a messy room. In this book, however, we will look for that treasured something with a clean slate. In *Self Discovery Journal*, we will first dispel all bondage to your past and any labels that may have been placed on you. Next, we will learn more about ourselves by understanding our preferences in the hierarchy of human needs. Afterward, we will assess our karmic cycles, so as to disassociate with any patterns that may be limiting us. Finally, we will go through 200 of the most powerful questions I've encountered to find out who we are and what we want in all eight areas of our lives.

Ready?

Welcome to *Self-Discovery Journal*.

Chapter One: Who I am NOT

"Someone's opinion of your does not have to become your reality."
-   *Les Brown*

Leslie Calvin Brown was abandoned in a deserted building upon birth, raised as an adoptive child by a single mother, and was labeled 'educable mentally retarded' in grammar school. He is someone that, by society's standards, we would not expect much from. Luckily for him (and the countless of people he's helped, including me), he chose not to buy into his past or into the labels he came across in his life.

'Les' Brown grew up with little self-esteem and even smaller belief in his possibilities. This was all changed upon meeting one of his first mentors, a teacher from school. This teacher would instill in his pupil the idea that he didn't have to follow the expectations others had of him. Once, Les was asked to do a math problem on the board during class.

"I can't do that sir", Les replied.

"Why not?" Asked his teacher.

"I'm educable mentally retarded, sir", Les confessed.

Les met his teacher's powerful gaze and was taken aback by the words that would follow.

"Son, don't let others' opinions of you become your reality".

This was to become Les's mantra for the rest of his life. Today, 'Les Brown' is synonymous with America's top motivational speaker. He's a man who has inspired hundreds of thousands of people through his talks, books and TV appearances. He's forged himself a legacy- all because he decided to release himself from his past and disassociate from labels placed upon him.

Do you feel that your past defines you?

Be honest with yourself here, real honest. If the answer is yes, then let me tell you that you're not alone. More people than you'd think have had their (insert tragic adjective here) pasts haunt them into living a life in reaction.

What's a life in a reaction like? It's when instead of choosing to quit your life-sucking day job and pursue your dreams, you accept the draining grind you find yourself in. It's simply when your mindset and decisions sprout from fear-based thoughts and paradigms.

If so, I need you to understand that you aren't alone. Most people are living in this paradigm, so don't be too harsh on yourself for it. Do know, however, that your past should neither weigh you down nor define your future.

I don't know what happened to you in the past. But I do know that it's time to let it go.

As a kid, I was an easy target for bullying. This wound up damaging my self-esteem growing up. I'd often feel inadequate or incapable in comparison to my peers.

As I aged into adulthood and learned about personal development, I found that I couldn't keep harboring these thoughts and resentment if I wanted to keep growing in life. I decided to let go of everything. Let go of a disempowered identity I had held, let go of built up emotions, let go of nearly everything that held me back. Though I'm far from done, I feel like I'm cruising through life lighter than ever.

I don't know much about you. But I do know that it's probably time that you also let go. By the way, if you need someone to chat with, you're welcome to hit me up at gerald@inwardthrive.com. I'll try to get back to you as soon as time allows!

How can you move forward and live in the present, when you can't let go of your past?

This sprouts from the premise that you can't let go of things. Well, you *can*.

Here are a few ideas you can incorporate to your daily living that will help you set yourself free:

1. *Change your perception and write a new story.* Instead of thinking about the past with anxiety or regret, think of your past as valuable life lessons you were meant to live to further improve yourself. If you have neglected your health, put on weight, got a divorce, broken up with your boyfriend or girlfriend, lied, hurt someone else, wasted your time, squandered away your finances or anything else, you can always realize that you are wiser now than you were in the past. You aren't the same person that you used to be and, therefore, you don't have to make the same mistakes again. Actually, you are evolving, maturing and learning from all your mistakes.

2. *Stop negative self-talk.* If our friends talked to us the same way we talk to ourselves, they probably wouldn't be our friends anymore. Stop punishing yourself for your past wrongdoings. If you are interested in making amends, then do so, but move forward.

Your Past Doesn't Define You and Neither Does Anything Else. You are Ever-Changing.

"Try to describe the scent of a rose with words. You can't. Then how can you attempt to describe the essence of a human?"
- *Unknown*

A human being can't be confined to be represented by a single word- it's just impossible. You are a dynamic person with different roles to play in life. Over the years, I've adopted the self-image of being a workaholic. However, I don't let this self-image stop me from spending time with my family and friends. I try to catch myself when I'm following a certain stereotype too closely. I don't want to a slave to ideas I have about myself. I invite you to do the same. You may love partying during weekends- and that's great! But don't fall into the mental trap of believing that you can't be a great professional or entrepreneur at the same time. The way the society perceives you (or the way you perceive yourself) shouldn't limit your thoughts and actions. The world classifies people based on their gender, sexual orientation, culture, race, or even their work. Don't expect these classifications to stop anytime soon. Understand this and proactively venture into your future based on what you want at this moment. Ultimately, this book is an invitation to carve an individuality for yourself.

Oh, and Beliefs Don't Define Your Either!
It is a popular misconception that your beliefs define you. We've all heard the Descartes saying, "I think therefore I am." However, I don't think this is entirely true.
The truth is, your beliefs are malleable. Every belief system under which you take action is something that can be changed.

How can this be true?
Well, you need not go far to realize this. As we mature in life, our beliefs about life evolve and change over time. I'm an example of this. Being the shy introvert that I was in my younger days, I would've thought it impossible for me to stand onstage to deliver a speech to 2000 people. I've done this now on multiple occasions. I certainly wasn't the "shy" person I thought I was years ago.

What exactly are your beliefs?
Beliefs are nothing more than assumptions about you and your surroundings that mold your actions. Our beliefs tend to arouse emotion and thus become the framework through which you experience life.

Are They Real?

Not necessarily. That's the tricky thing about beliefs. Our minds see them as absolute truths when most of the time they're not. Many of our beliefs are actually holding us back.

For instance, when little Tom is scolded for speaking up in class, he learns at an early age that talking loudly or speaking back will get him in trouble. Tom is 30 years old now and has trouble communicating discord or facing conflict. Tom feels worthless because he lacks the 'spine' to communicate his side of the story during arguments. Why? Deep down, he still believes he will get scolded for it.

Making Them Conscious

Beliefs such as these are *limiting* beliefs and are therefore undesirable. To get rid of them, we must first identify them. Thus, we enter one of the most enlightening areas of self-discovery, which focuses on understanding and overcoming the beliefs that have held us back for years.

Take a sheet of paper and list down some of the beliefs that you have formed in your mind and you have accepted to be true. You might not believe in some of these views at a consciously level, you may have them at a subconscious one. Here are a few examples:
- *I will never be good enough.*
- *I am really not that important.*
- *I am simply not smart enough.*
- *I will never be able to do anything well.*
- *No one takes me seriously.*
- *I am useless, I am unlucky, I am undeserving.*
- *I am not good looking, no one will ever love me.*
- *I am too old, or I am too young...*
- And so on... The list is endless.

Find Where They Originated

Once you've written all the beliefs you think have held you back, I'd considering asking yourself: *where did this belief originate?* Write away.

Belief-Buster!

Now what? *Prove your belief wrong.* For instance, if you think you're too short to deserve love, then go ahead and google short celebrities dating hotties, improve your dating life, find ways to make short sexy. I'm sure you'll come up with many. Eventually, this limiting belief will be no more.

Existential Question: If I'm Not My Beliefs, What Am I?

That's a great question for which I don't really have an answer. I try to stand by the saying *'Trust those who seek the answers, questions those who claim to have found them'*. So, I'm not going to go all philosophical on you and impose an answer to a question that has boggled the brightest minds in history. However, I will give a suggestion that has worked for me: *live your life according to what feels rights*. Every day try to live more, experience more and *feel* more. While it's tough to say who we are, it's relatively easy to identify what we are not. And we're definitely not the incessant, negative, obsessive chatter in our heads that prevents us from living in the present moment.

Here's a suggestion for further reading about who you really are. A lot of the New Age Spirituality ethos revolves around finding oneself in the absence of noise, e.g. meditation, and I love it. Spirituality guru Eckhart Tolle shares with us that people have two 'selves' within them. Take as an example the last time you said, "I can't stand myself." This statement implies that there exists a duality within us. A self that acts, and a self that experiences the other's actions. This 'self' which experiences the actions of the other is who we really are- consciousness experiencing a human mental image of the world. That's about the finest existential definition I've found of who we are. However, it's something I recommend reading and experiencing on your own. By the way, the book's name is *The Power of Now*.

Chapter Two: Who I am

Have you watched 'Kung Fu Panda 3'? There is a particular scene in this movie that strung a chord with me. Towards the end of the movie, the protagonist, Po (yes, the panda) figures out who he is. He realizes that he plays different roles in his life and he is an amalgamation of all those parts. This is just about the best definition of *who you are* I can deliver on this book without seeming too pretentious.

So, "Who am I?"
You may be a parent, a friend, a spouse, an accountant, a doctor, a traveler, a patient or anything else. The truth is, you are a parent because you have a child. You are a husband or a wife because you are married. You are a traveler because you are on a journey. So, we all have different roles and identities, don't we? The task is to find the common essence found in all of these roles and identities.

How to Find Our Essence Among the Roles We Play
There are six building blocks of self-knowledge, and these are Values, Interests, Temperament, Around-the-clock activities, Life, and Strengths. It can all be summed up in the acronym VITALS. These VITALS make up what you've come to know subconsciously as your sense of identity. They literally make you *you*. Considering your VITALS will make your answers to the upcoming 200 questions that much more profound. So, let's begin!

Values

What things in life do you value? Out of those which values do you give more priority to? Your values could be anything like helping others, creativity, financial stability, staying healthy and so on. Now ask yourself, *what do you value most?* Answering these questions will provide you with an ampler understanding of yourself.

By becoming conscious of your values, you will understand why you take the actions you take, what core motivations drive you, and the pillars over which you will build your life. *E.g. You could be an introvert, but if you value leaving your comfort zone over self-expression, you may find yourself attempting public speaking over expressing yourself through writing. And that's completely fine.*

Interests

Interests would include anything that can retain your attention over prolonged periods of time. Your interests can include all the things you are passionate about, your hobbies, or anything else that you find interesting.

There are a couple of questions that you can ask yourself for deciding what your interests are. What are the things that you usually pay attention to? What ignites your curiosity? What are your concerns? Your life will become quite vivid when you can focus your mental energy on something that excites and interests you. Understanding your interests will provide you with clues about the things that you are genuinely passionate about. All the people who are successful have found their success by doing things that interest them. If you aren't interested in something, then it is highly unlikely that you will spend any time or energy working on it.

Temperament

Temperament refers to your natural preferences. Do you feel you are more of an introvert or an extrovert? Do you thrive in social situations or does it just make you feel exhausted? Do you like planning for things or do you wish to take things as they come your way? Are you concerned with the minor details or do you like big ideas?

The answers to these questions will help you in realizing the situations that will help you prosper. It will also help you in understanding all those things that you should ignore. There are some who like to be spontaneous, and then there are those who love to plan and then act deliberately. For instance, in the present world, spontaneity seems to be more valuable than planning. However, you don't have to opt for one over the other just because of the opinions that others hold. It is okay to go against the societal norm if it means that you are doing something that goes well with your personality. It is okay to be a planner if that is what you are comfortable with. The key to understanding yourself is acceptance.

Around the clock activities

What activities have you surrounded your daily grind with? Any repeated action becomes a habit, which eventually becomes something your end up building an identity around. What activities compose your life?

Make sure that the activities you engage in daily are making out of you what you actually want to become.

Life mission

What would you do for the rest of your life even if you weren't a paid a dime for it? What would you regret not having done if you were to die today?

Think of your past. Remember what you wished to accomplish as a child, for instance. By recollecting such fond memories, you can get an idea of what you'd like to devote your life to. It is never too late to do something different, as long as it means that you are doing something that you like. Take some time and give it a real thought. It will help you in understanding yourself in a better manner.

Still unsure? I recommend checking out my book, *Find Your Passion*.

Find it on Amazon here: http://bit.ly/FindYourPassionAMZ

Strengths

What activity or thing do people ask you for help in? What abilities do you deem you're good at? What would others say you're good at?

Your strengths include your abilities, skills, and talents, but aren't necessarily restricted to just that. For instance, your characteristic traits like loyalty, comprehension, inclination towards learning, your IQ and EQ are all examples of possible strengths. Learn and grow your strengths so that you strengthen your sense of individuality.

Chapter Three: What We All Want

We've got our VITALS down. The way we adhere to our VITALS is what makes use unique. There are, however, human needs that make us all similar- despite how different our VITALS may be between one another. This chapter is dedicated to bringing light to the human needs we all share and how you're going about fulfilling them (and in which order of priority!). Let's get started!

Certainty or comfort

The most basic human need is the need for comfort or assurance. It's near impossible to live life in complete uncertainty. Imagine not knowing whether you'll be alive or have enough food to make it through the day tomorrow. To find ourselves in an optimal state, we need to feel certainty that our present has a certain stability.

This need dictates the level of risk you are willing to take in different aspects of your life, like your job, in investments, and even our relationships. The higher the need for certainty, fewer are the risks you will be willing to take or experience emotionally.

How much do you value certainty and comfort in your life?

Uncertainty or variety

The second need is the need for variety or even a little uncertainty in life. It might sound in direct contradiction of the first requirement. However, haven't you heard the age-old adage, *'variety is the spice of life'*? Well, it's certainly true. Monotony kills and it's the reason why people love traveling, meeting new people, starting new things, etc.

Embracing uncertainty is also a requirement for growth. Think about it-everything that you don't know and want to learn about is outside of your zone of comfort. Therefore, to keep learning and growing in life, we must be able to thrive in variety.

How much do you embrace variety and uncertainty in your life? If having more of it in your life meant more growth and fulfillment, would you be willing to further open up to uncertainty?

Significance

Who doesn't like feeling special, unique, or even needed? If your answer is *'not me'*, then you are kidding yourself. We all want to feel special one way or another. I would even argue that if you answered with *'not me'*, that in itself may be showing your need to feel special or different from the rest.

However, the question is, how do you get that significance you are looking for? You can achieve it by earning a lot of money, collecting degrees, or even by building a significant social media presence. How are you getting yours?

Love and connection

All we need is love, right? Well, it's not the only thing, but it's certainly one of them. Love is an essential human need. It is a gift of life and unsurprisingly, it's one of the things that make you feel the most alive. Be careful with this one though. Because of how badly people pursue romantic love, most are willing to settle for connection when they can't find it. And settling for connection like settling for the cookies crumbs of love's box full of cookies- at least in the case of romance.

Keep in mind that love is expressed in a romantic manner as well as in a non-romantic manner. Don't lose sight of connections and bonds with friends and family. They're also equally important in what makes up our lives.

Is your need for love being met? Are you settling for only connection at a romantic level? How close are you keeping your friends and family?

Growth

Whatever isn't growing is dying, it's a fact of life. One of our greatest drives as human beings is to expand our sphere of influence, our skills, and grow through our endeavors. If there is no growth in a relationship, your career, or anything else, you are slowly dying (not in a literal sense, obviously).

You may already be rich, healthy, have a wonderful life partner and family, but if you're not growing in any of these areas of your life, you will stagnant. It's not about being greedy, it's about understanding the needs of your psyche.

Have you been devoting time to your growth lately? What priority does growth have in your life?

Contribution

One need that sounds quite clichéd is the need for contribution. Take a moment and think about the bigger picture. Life is so much more than about yourself. Life is about all of us. What is the first thing you do whenever you receive good news or when something good happens to you? It is quite likely that you are eager to share that piece of happiness with someone you love. Sharing enriches the entire experience. Life is about creating meaning, and it doesn't come from whatever you get, it arises when you start giving. It is not about what you get that will make you happy, but rather who you are as a person, and what you have managed to contribute.

Have you been contributing lately? Or have you been too stuck in your head lately (it happens to all of us!)?

Take the time to find your hierarchy. Which of the human needs do you value the most?

There are six basic needs, and each of these requirements holds a different place in the lives of various individuals. What might be considered to be very important for me might not mean the same for someone else. If significance is my most important need, then the way I make decisions will be different from someone for whom love is an essential need. It is essential to understand this.

Here's a small exercise for you. Rate yourself depending on how important each one of these needs is to you on a scale from 1 to 5, with 1 being not important at all and 5 being extremely important. What is your biggest need? What need do you pay the least attention to? What've you learned from doing this?

Chapter Four: Recognizing Karmic Cycles and What You Want

To fully understand yourself, the last thing I'd suggest you do is to identify your karmic cycles. Understanding your karmic cycles will help you see why you are experiencing what you're experiencing.

What are Karmic Cycles?

What I've found over the years is that life has a funny way of teaching us things. If we've got a lesson to learn, life will make sure we'll keep reliving experiences from which we should learn this lesson. And until we've learned it, we're doomed to keep re-living similar experiences. I know this sounds a bit woo-woo, but just hear me out for a second. Have you watched the movie Groundhog Day? In the film, when Bill Murray realizes that he is living the same day over and over, he comes up with the idea that helps him fixing things that previously went wrong. He managed to understand how he could fix the relationship with the object of his love. He even came up with a better manner of dealing with the incredibly annoying insurance salesman who kept approaching him daily. Only when he learned to accept his fate and made peace with himself, did the day end for him. This is the best analogy I can come up with for explaining what a karmic cycle is.

For Instance…

Say you've always had bad experiences choosing romantic partners. They always end up leaving you one way or another. Then, finally, you meet the one. He or she is perfect in every single sense. But, as you're courting him or her you can't help but feel a sense of déjà vu. Subconsciously, you know that they will end up leaving you. The romance comes and goes, and you realize that it was true!

This used to happen to me all the time! I always fell for a girl that I knew I couldn't be with long-term. Either the girl was a tourist or exchange student, or she was someone whom I'd have to leave because I had to relocate soon. Subconsciously, it's what I wanted and searched for in a girl.

In What Aspect of Your Life Are You Living in Karmic Cycles?

Take some time and reflect on your life. Do you feel like you are reliving the same karmic cycles over and over again? It doesn't have to be in relationships alone. It could be in any other aspect of your life like your work. Have you ever faced the same problem at work that seems to keep coming back in different disguises?

The situation is going to continue repeating itself until you become conscious of it, take away the lesson you should learn from it and take a course of action different from what you'd normally take. This is the only way of dispelling this groundhog day-like spell.

You Are Not Your Karmic Cycles

We pretty much established this already but it's worth repeating. Once you become conscious of them, karmic cycles that may have defined you in the past and formed part of your identity completely dissolve. Thus, the fake identity built around them also dissolves. Don't associate with karmic cycles or form generalizations around them. Saying things such as *'I'm just not good at love'* is not only inaccurate but further hides the fact that you've got a karmic cycle you need to dispel.

Chapter Five: Areas of Your Life and Important Questions

We can finally get to the main part of this book. By now we have:
- Disassociated with our past, examined our labels and even questioned our beliefs.
- Understood that our inner essence can be best defined by looking into your preferences and longings.
- As part of understanding our preferences and longings we have looked at our VITALS and the 6 Basic Human Needs
- We have learned about karmic cycles and have disassociated from them.

With these heaps of knowledge, we can finally address the 200 questions of self-discovery. To better organize these questions, I have divided them into 8 areas: Health, Wealth, Family and Friends, Playtime/Hobbies, Relationships, Career/Job/Business, Mind and Emotions, and Contribution/Spirituality.

Please take your time through them. It's not a race. Quite the opposite, the longer you take answering these questions, the more fulfilled you'll be.
- Start with the area of your life that you want to focus on and answer these questions with a clean slate.
- Answer the question thoroughly. There is really no limit to how long the answer may be. Let the answer flow from your essence. If you have the physical copy of this book and feel the space is too small, please use a separate piece of paper.
- As you're writing, take into consideration your VITALS and your preference in the hierarchy of human needs. Disassociate from your past, from labels and from any negative karmic cycles that may be limiting your aspirations. Allow your dreams and longings complete freedom to express themselves in the answers.

- Make sure you come back to continue this process of self-discovery. Self-discovery is a lifelong process, as you're a human being that is in constant evolution. These questions will, however, guide you through every step of that evolution.

Self Discovery Questions on Health

Physical health

1. **My definition**

   What is my definition of healthy? What words, thoughts, and feelings have I associated around the word *health*?

2. **Let's talk 'sickness'.**

   What words, thoughts, and feelings have I associated around this word? Am I a sickly person? Why or why not?

3. **Creating a roadmap**

   Where am I in terms of physical health? Where do I want to be? What's my ideal body or physical state like? Write away.

4. **Roadblocks**

   What's stopping me from getting there?

5. **Love what you do**

   If I had to choose my favorite physical activity, it'd have to be.... Because.... (Please no eating, sleeping, etc....you get the point)

6. **Physicality and I**

Am I a physically active person? Why or why not? What're some physical activities that you hate?

7. **Do more**

How can I start doing more? There's something regarding your health you should be doing more of. Now's the time to identify what.

8. **You are what you eat**

   Describe the top 5 foods that you eat most often. Next, rate each of the foods you've written about on a scale from 1 to 5, with 1 being very unhealthy and 5 being very healthy. How healthy are your eating habits?

9. **Time for a hate list.**

   List down all the foods you hate to eat. Next, like before, rate each of them on a scale from 1 to 5, with 1 being unhealthy and 5 being healthy. Found any correlations?

10. **The ideal list.**

Make a list of all the foods you love and are also healthy. How can you get yourself to start eating more of these?

11. **The health mastermind**

Where can you find people that have the body and health you'd want to have? Describe how spending time with them would radically change your physical state. Next, go out and find them.

12. **Activity evaluation**

   Make a list of all the activities you engage in throughout the day. Which of these activities add to your health? Which of them take away from your health?

13. **A message to yourself**

   Recall a time you've tried to improve your physical health and eventually talked yourself out of it. What would you like to say to your past self?

14. A writing prompt

My body is…

15. Limited no more

Jot down limiting beliefs you may have about health and wellbeing (*e.g. I'm overweight because that's just the way I am*). Next, write an action you could take to prove these beliefs wrong.

16. **The pursuit of happiness**

    How do I define happiness in my life? What is preventing me from being happy right now? How can I make happiness as normal as breathing?

17. **Thought evaluation**

    What are the negative thoughts that keep recurring in my head? What triggers these thoughts? What are the positive thoughts that keep me happy? What triggers these thoughts?

18. Making the shift

How can I try to keep out negative thoughts and keep my mind full of positive thoughts? Is meditation an option?

19. My friend Fear

We're all running from something one way or another. What's one thing you could be afraid of and are running away from?

20. **Giver of meaning**

Describe things that have happened to you that left a negative mark on you. Is there a way you could see those things in a positive light? If the saying *every cloud has a silver lining* were true, how could it apply to the negative things you've experienced?

21. **Worrisome Worries**

Do you worry often? Describe a time in the past where you worried yourself senseless for something you forgot about a few days after.

22. **No one's perfect**

Recall a mistake you made that you still haven't forgiven yourself for. Write yourself an action plan for moving on.

23. **Forgive thyself**

Write a letter from your future self to your present self forgiving you for what you've done.

24. Forgiving Others

Write a letter to those who've wronged you. If forgiving them meant moving on, would you do it?

25. Inner chatter

What thoughts keep me awake at night? List them down and label them as either positive or negative.

Self-Discovery Questions on Wealth

1. **Money, money, money...**
   Define wealth in your own words. According to you, is wealth good or bad? Do you want it or is it something that repels you?

2. **Judging wealth**
   There are wealthy people that are good and donate millions of dollars to worthy causes and work towards the advancement of humanity. Likewise, there are wealthy people that are despicable and deserve little of what they have. If you were wealthy, which would you be? What would you do with your money?

3. **If you had all the time and money in the world...**
   What would you do?

4. **Wealth is good when in good hands**
   Wealth can be good when it provides security, when it gives you and those around you freedom of time, and when it's used to provide jobs for others. Taking this into consideration, is generating wealth a priority in your life? Am I comfortable with this place of priority?

5. **How much do you need?**

   Have a serious look at your finances. How much money would you need to make per month to live comfortably, provide security for you and those around you, and have the freedom to do the things you've always wanted to do?

6. **Wealthblocks**

   What is stopping me from achieving my desired wealth? Is it mindset? Lack of motivation? Not knowing where to start?

7. **The wrong way to make money**

Are my wealth-creating methods misaligned with my life mission? *E.g. people who can't fathom a life without the piano but are stuck serving customers at a bank.*

8. **On mastery**

What skills help me earn my income? What other skills do I have that I can monetize?

9. **Sharpen your blade**

   What skills do I need to learn to earn more money?

10. **Monetizing your passion**

    It's not something limited to millennials with social media
    followings. You can do it too! Can I convert my passions into a
    wealth-creating profession? If it were possible, would it worth
    dedicating at least a few hours a day to this pursuit?

11. Looking for Yoda

How can you go about finding someone who has already generated wealth or has monetized their passion? How can you start learning from them?

12. On investing

What are the available investment opportunities that will help me get returns and increase my wealth over time? What's stopping me from learning about these opportunities?

13. **Bless what you want**

    Does it affect me if my colleague or neighbor or someone else earns more money than I do? Do I befriend them, and endeavor to learn from them? Or do I look at them in envy and ridicule their success?

14. **How bad do you want it?**

    What amount of time do I spend on wealth creation each day? Is making money a large part of my around-the-clock activities? Remember, action expresses priority.

15. The chicken or the egg?

What should take priority, your passion or the way you make money?

16. A money affair

What's your relationship with money? Do you spend it all as soon as it lands in your pocket? Or do you save most of it and live below your means?

17. Money memories

Describe your parents' (or guardians') money habits. Did they always fight about money? Or was money something abundant during your childhood? How do you this affected your view of money?

18. Debt conciliator

We have to make money an important part of our lives if we want to have it in abundance. Make a list of all the people that owe you money and haven't paid you back and make a list of all the people you've borrowed money from but haven't paid back. Which are you more likely to do, borrow or lend? Do you think it's about time to conciliate these debts?

19. **#financialgoals**

Do I have my financial goals in place? What are your financial goals for this and the following five years?

20. **The richest man in Babylon**

The secret to wealth building? Save up 10 percent of everything that goes into your pockets for future investing. Write down a plan that will help you save a dime of every dollar you earn. If that's too much, then start with a nickel.

21. Financial Denial

Am I keeping my financial problems hidden from others who can help me? Am I in denial of my money problems?

22. Mind over money

It's important not to focus so much on wealth creation to the point that you disregard completely every other area of your life. Describe a life in which you're hustling and making money while winning in other areas of your life simultaneously. What needs to happen?

23. Tracking money

For the next 7 days, jot down every penny you spend throughout the day. It will show you just how much of a spender you really are.

24. Money wisdom

What's the worst financial advice you've heard? What's the best financial advice you've heard? Why?

25. I deserve money and abundance in my life because...

Go ahead, write away.

Self Discovery Questions on Family and Friends

1. **Family, Friends, and Priorities**

   What value do I place on my family and friends? What priority does it hold in comparison to the other areas of my life? *E.g. If I was called to work on a weekend during which there is a very important family function already planned, will I find the courage to say no to my boss?*

2. **Sharing love**

   Describe how you share your love with your family and friends. When was the last time you made them feel special?

3. **Back to my roots**

   Where does your family come from? What is your ancestry like? How has this affected the way you were raised?

4. **Family values**

   What main values did your parents strive to instill in you? Do you still hold these values close to you? What're your thoughts on them?

5. **Lessons from siblings**

   Describe a very important life lesson learned from a sibling or cousin (if you're an only child).

6. **Know thy parents**

   What do your parents love and appreciate?

7. **Bonding efforts**

   What can you do to spend more *quality* time with your friends and family?

8. **Childhood memories**

   Describe your happiest childhood memory. What made this so special?

9. **Childhood memories part 2**

   Describe a sad memory from your childhood. Were you able to overcome it?

10. **3 words**

   Use three words to describe your family. Use three words to describe your friends. Did you find any similarities?

11. **On legacy**

   What legacy will your parents leave behind after they pass? What legacy do you want to leave behind for your children?

12. Hardships forge bonds

What was the largest hardship your family overcame together? What did you learn from this?

13. Opening up

How open do you want your children to be with you as they grow up? How open have you been with your parents?

14. **Dad**

   If you had to pinpoint the biggest lesson taught to you by your dad, what would it be? If you didn't have a dad present in your life, then you can use any male figure.

15. **Mom**

   If you had to pinpoint the biggest lesson taught to you by your mom, what would it be? If you didn't have a mom present in your life, then you can use any female figure.

16. Revisiting bedtime stories

What was the bedtime story you remember hearing the most as a child? How do you think this story affected your view of the world?

17. Attitude reflections

Describe how you act when surrounded by superiors. Next, describe how you act around your parents. Is your attitude similar or different? What could this indicate?

18. A family memory

Describe the first memory you have of being with your family. I know it's blurry, but you can do it!

19. On gratitude

What are three things about your family you are grateful for?

20. Sibling love

You all are probably all grown up. What do you miss the most about spending time with your siblings as a child?

21. What about friends?

Who are my close friends? List their names and describe why they mean so much to you.

22. Friendly expectations

Do my friends expect something from our friendship? Do I expect anything from our friendship?

23. The ingredients of friendship

What activities do I enjoy the most in the company of my friends? Is there something special to bond us together?

24. **BFFs**

Who do I consider my best friend? Why? What am I willing to do for him or her?

25. **Are you a friend you'd like to have?**

Open-ended. Answer your heart out.

Self Discovery Questions on Playtime/Hobbies

1. **Playtime priority**

   What value do I attach to the personal time in which I follow my hobbies? Am I allowing myself enough time to indulge in hobbies?

2. **On catching up**

   How often do you catch up with friends? Spending time with good friends heals the heart. Make sure to do it often.

3. **Thoughts of socializing**

   400 words or less. Go!

4. **Project U**

   How would I describe a perfect weekend?'

5. **Make a List**

   What are your hobbies? What are the activities that fill you with life again?

6. **Socially savvy vs insta savvy**

   What are your thoughts on spending time socializing through social media vs real life interactions?

7. **But what if...**

   I watch a lot of TV in my free time. Does that mean watching TV is my hobby? How can I better use my playtime to help me lead a fulfilled and happy life?

8. **Reward yourself**

   When was the last time you rewarded yourself for all your hard work? How often do you indulge in me-time?

9. **Fun**

   Write all the words, emotions, activities and mental images associated with this amazing word.

10. Hobby hunting

Always wanted to try something new? Make a list of all the things you could be spending your time on.

11. Opening up during play

Do you feel self-conscious when you go out to play? Or are you able to get yourself to enjoy it?

12. A writing assignment

What's something you've always wanted to write about?

13. Paint it, pin it

I know there's something you've always wanted to draw but put off for the future. Now's the time to do it. Draw it and put it somewhere you can see it.

14. **Traveling the world**

Where do you want to travel? Make a list and choose your next vacation destination.

15. **Lose yourself**

When was the last time I got so involved in something I completely lost track of time and even forgot to eat?

16. Life's a game

If life were a game, how would you play it? Is this different from how you've been *'playing'* your life until now?

17. Childhood dream

As a kid, what did you dream about doing for fun?

18. **Embrace uncertainty**

   Go out today (or as soon as time allows) without an itinerary to the first place that crosses your mind. Have the most fun you can have and make sure to journal about it in the space below.

19. **Dancing King/Queen**

   No matter your gender, everyone could use a dancing lesson or two. If you had to pick a dancing genre to learn, which would it be? Why?

20. **In the pursuit of awkward**

What's a fun activity others enjoy that you could never wrap your head around doing? Do it and journal about it below.

21. **Maker of anecdotes**

For one day, pursue actions that would make for great anecdotes. *E.g. Chat up a random stranger on the streets, post an embarrassing Instagram photo, sing in public, etc.*

22. Your finest hour

Craft the speech of your life. Do so below.

23. We all have that friend

We all have a friend that's crazier than the norm. Spend a day with him or her and give in to the madness. Then, proceed to journal about it.

24. **Budgeting Hobbies**

A great book on money habits called *The Secrets of the Millionaire Mind* recommends that we separate a small percentage (5-10%) of what we earn exclusively for hobbies and fun. How much of your money are you spending on fun? Is it within the healthy range mentioned above?

25. **Say yes!**

Say yes to the next times you're asked to try out something different or new. Journal about it below.

Self-Discovery Questions on Relationships

1. **Love priorities**

   What value do I give to my relationships in my life?

2. **What you really want**

   Often relationships can get messy because we don't know what we want. Are you currently in search of long-term love? Short-term flings? A sense of security? Someone to keep you company? Describe your ideal love at this point in your life.

3. **What do you value more in relationships?**

   Stability or freedom? How does this affect your relationships?

4. **Scary love**

   What do you find scary about falling in love? Why?

5. **This one requires raw honesty**

   Describe your ideal relationship. Describe your ideal other half.
   Describe your ideal self with your ideal other half.

6. **On compliments**

   On a scale from 1 to 10, how open are you to receiving compliments? How about your partner?

7. **Need some air!**

   Have you ever felt suffocated in a relationship? What happened to make you feel that way?

8. **The perfect couple**

   Who are my role models when it comes to maintaining perfect relationships? What do they do that I should replicate?

9. **Eek!**

   Who are the people whose relationship methods I definitely do not want to follow? What are they doing wrong?

10. What is love?

Thoroughly describe it.

11. Abuse

Was I a victim of abuse in my childhood? Unless you've worked through this with a therapist, it may still be affecting your present relationships. Have you received the necessary help to overcome those problems?

12. **Learning from our parents**

    How was the relationship between my parents? Describe all the things you loved about your parents' relationship that you'd like to replicate in your own.

13. **Relationship solutions inc.**

    If I face any kind of disagreement in a relationship, how do I handle it? How can I improve the way I solve conflict with my partner?

14. On expression

What's the best way to express negative emotions? Why?

15. Feeling the love

Do you know what kind of behavior makes you feel loved and appreciated? Describe in detail 3 moments when your partner made you feel loved.

16. **What's the most important lesson...**

    I want to teach my children about finding love?

17. **Unnoticed hurting**

    Recall a time you said something and unknowingly hurt your partner for it. How can you avoid this in the future? Likewise, what kind of comments hurt you when you hear them from your significant other?

18. **We all need space sometimes**

    Jot down the perfect strategy for balancing out me-time with us-time.

19. **Money, baby**

    How is wealth handled in your relationship? Describe the ideal way money should be administered in the relationship you want at this moment.

20. **Loving myself first**

How can you tell when you're searching for a relationship only to fill a void within yourself?

21. **Family opinions**

How important is your family in choosing your significant other? Why?

22. Loving jealousy

Am I proud of my partner's achievements? Or have I secretly held envy for their accomplishments?

23. Dumping your ex, again.

Describe your relationship with your ex. Is having him around holding you back from moving on?

24. **A healing recipe**

Describe how you go about healing from a broken heart... or a broken relationship.

25. **It's always time to begin anew**

Is it about time you started anew? *Note that you can start anew with the same person.*

Self-Discovery Questions on Career/Job/Business

1. **A matter of priorities**

   How important is the career/job/business area of my life? How does it rank compared to other areas? Why?

2. **On the daily grind**

   How do I feel about my daily routine? If money was not a problem, would I continue to be doing the same things I am doing now?

3. **Define career/business success**

   What does success mean to you? Under your own definition, rate yourself in terms of success in a scale from 1 to 5.

4. **Why?**

    Why did you rate yourself a (insert rating here) in success?

5. **Success hypothesis**

    I can be more successful if I improve my… and if I limit my…

6. **No 'I' in team**

Thoughts on being a team player. Are you one?

7. **Do more, work less**

What should you be delegating right now?

8. **My success blueprint**

   Make a list of all the skills necessary to have massive success in your career or business. Describe what you can do to incorporate more of them in your life.

9. **Millionaire Mentor**

   Find one. Every industry has one. Where can you find a mentor that can show you the steps required to making it to the top?

10. Looking ahead

What do you visualize yourself doing 5 years from now? What about 10? You'll know you're doing something wrong if these two questions don't excite you.

11. Catch 'em while you can

What opportunities are passing you by?

12. Career legacy

From a career perspective, how would I like to be remembered? For example, if I quit today, what are the things I imagine people are missing me for?

13. Looking back...

When I am over 60, what will I regret not doing the most career-wise?

14. Idea listing!

Think about career or business ideas you've had and always wanted to implement. Make a list of them.

15. If you were fired tomorrow...

and could choose any other job or career path, what would it be?

16. Accomplishments

When I look back at my career until now, do I feel happy and satisfied with what I have done and achieved?

17. On my mojo

Describe the peak moments in your career. What has to happen to reach another peak?

18. Think possibilities

Is there something you want to attempt, even if failure was certain?

19. Let me rephrase that

What would you do career or business-wise, if you knew with certainty that you could not fail? What are you waiting for to get started?

20. **A (wo)man's search for passion**
    What are the activities I get involved in so much that I completely lose track of time and feel refreshed even after spending long hours doing?

21. **Your hidden genius!**
    What skills do I have that are so natural in my mind and body that I believe everyone can do it as easily as I can?

22. Personal expertise

What are the subjects that I can talk about or discuss for a long period of time without feeling bored or tired? What subjects inspire me?

23. Thirsty for knowledge

What subject or topic could you learn incessantly about and still want more?

24. A letter from my older self

If your older self were to give you career advice, what would he or she say?

25. Inner circle

Having a robust and thriving inner circle is necessary for long-term success. Describe how you're going about creating your inner circle.

Self-Discovery Questions on Mind and Emotions

1. **Mindset maintenance**

   What are you feeding your mind? What kind of content are you consuming through your newsfeed and social media? Do you think it affects the way you think?

2. **A beautiful mind**

   What priority do you place on working on your mindset and emotions? How does this compare to other areas of our life?

3. **The willpower pill**

   If you could get yourself to have an willpower on demand, what's the first thing you'd try to get done?

4. **The willpower recipe**

   What has to happen for you to draw in enough willpower to get things done? Is it something you control or others control for you?

5. **Mind over matter**

   Recall a time you pushed through adversity on sheer determination. How did it feel?

6. **Your hidden superpower**

   There's no hiding it. Mindset, willpower, and determination are a choice. What will you choose to devote all of your mental capacity to?

7. **"What the mind can believe...**

   It can achieve", or so it was said by the late success expert Napoleon Hill. Share your thoughts on this.

8. **Emotional declutter**

   Crying is a great way to let go of emotions. It is said to cleanse the soul. Is this wishy-washy self-help bull? Or a gem of wisdom we've all forgotten?

9. **Stress and I**

   Describe your relationship with our friend Stress and how you cope with her.

10. Dumping stress

There's no escaping stress. In a sense, it's an indicator that we're alive. How can you learn to live with and accept her while you go on with your life?

11. Positivity contagion

Design a plan for spreading positivity wherever you go.

12. **Hello, I am good enough**

You're good enough. I'm good enough. We're all good enough. How does it feel to be good enough?

13. **Kindly**

Jot down three reasons people deserve to be treated kindly even if you don't know them.

14. Emotional growth

On a scale from 1 to 10, how well do you manage your emotions today? How well did you manage them 5 years ago? Have you seen an improvement?

15. Emotions hurt!

Sometimes, opening yourself up to others hurts and many decide to shut away their feelings (men, I'm looking at you). Write on why you should open up to others regardless.

16. Giver of hope

How do you give yourself hope in times of crisis and gloom?

17. Courageous U

Describe a moment in which you were courageous and stood by your beliefs.

18. Making amends

Similar to what we did before, write a short letter of apology to those you've wronged.

19. Emotional Mastery

What emotions are holding you back? How you can you let go of them?

20. **Radical acceptance**

Write a letter to yourself accepting every little nuance about you (be it positive or negative).

21. **Perfect imperfection**

Being perfect is for losers. Jot down all the reasons you're not perfect, and make sure to do it with pride.

22. Self-esteem

What's a clear sign you're acting out of self-love?

23. Self-love

How can you show more self-love to yourself?

24. **Breathe in the air**

Next time you're put in a tough spot, stop for a second and take a deep breath. Slowly exhale as you think of your response. Document your findings here.

25. **Every day, in every way...**

I'm getting better and better. List 3 reasons as to why this is true!

Self-Discovery Questions on Contribution or Spirituality

1. **Spirituality defined**

   How do you define spirituality? Journal about a time when you felt a spiritual connection.

2. **I feel spiritual when…**

   Complete the writing prompt.

3. **Eightfold path**

   Is there a particular path you're following towards spiritual enlightenment (*e.g. a religion*)? Why does this path resonate with you?

4. **Coherence**

   How strictly are you abiding by your chosen spiritual path?

5. **Open minds begin with open hearts**

   Do you think people of different creeds or spiritual beliefs should be able to get along with each other? Why or why not?

6. **Rules for spirituality?**

Do you believe spirituality should feel intuitive or should it be doctrine with rules you should follow? Is it, perhaps, a combination of both?

7. **Spiritually you**

What do you do to feel a spiritual connection with others and with the world around you?

8. **Contribution defined**

   How do you define contribution? Jot down your thoughts on it and why you think not many people go out of their way to help others.

9. **How I can contribute**

   The cause that I would like to contribute to the most is… because…

10. **Money and spirituality**

Money is easily the most emotionally-charged object in existence and circulates through nearly all humans. What are your thoughts on this mechanism and its relationship with matters of the spirit?

11. **Growing in spirit**

How do you see yourself spiritually a few years from now?

12. Spirituality in the now

Many modern spirituality gurus dictate that a higher consciousness is accessible only to do those who live in the present and in the now. What are your thoughts on this?

13. Praying mantras

Is praying an integral part of your spiritual growth? If so, jot down a prayer you'd like to recite more often.

14. **Right and wrong**

What is more important to me; to do the right things or do things in the right manner?

15. **Nature spirit**

There's a tacit agreement between us humans that nature is also important in a spiritual sense. Describe an instance in which you felt soothed and at ease in nature.

16. **On morality**

    What are my thoughts on morality and immorality? Is immorality ever justifiable?

17. **Spirit science!**

    Make a list of all the spirituality books you've read, those you're currently reading, and those you'd love to read!

18. Blind faith

Share your thoughts on it in 400 words or less.

19. Miracle worker

What are miracles for you? Do you believe in them?

20. Absolute good and evil

Do absolute truths exist? What is your notion of good and evil?

21. A lotus flower

Have you ever tried meditating? Do you feel meditation can be a vehicle for spiritual growth? Why?

22. ...And justice for all

Define the word *freedom*.

23. If you had 5 minutes with God...

What questions would you ask the Almighty?

24. **Detaching yourself from everything**

Many people believe that to grow spirituality you must detach yourself from the material world. What're your thoughts on this? Is it possible to be spiritual and live in the material world at the same time?

25. **I want to be happy when I'm older**

Describe your kind of spirituality. One that makes you and others happy. One that feels intuitive and correct. Make sure to live it every day of your life.

26. **When should you look away?**

Is it ever correct to turn a blind eye when you come across a less fortunate individual asking for help?

27. **Changing the world**

Create a recipe for changing the world. What should you and others do?

28. Fill your own cup first

Many self-help experts believe you should only help others when your cup is already full and is overflowing. That is, when you've already helped yourself first. What are your thoughts on this?

29. Ephemeral

In the end, our lives are but tiny specks of time in the infinite continuum that is the universe. Do you believe we uphold an undeserved importance about ourselves?

30. On life after death

Describe your thoughts on this long-debated topic.

31. Reflections

'Life is God's gift to each one of us. The way we live our lives is our gift to God' This is a saying that resonated with me since I first heard it a few years ago. What're your thoughts on it?

A Short Conclusion

Our ability for self-reflection is one of the gifts of life. Thank you for taking the time to do so through this journal. My hope is that you've found yourself through your writing and that this may lead to a more fulfilled life. Thank you and bless you.

Liked This Book?

If you've enjoyed *Self Discovery Journal: 200 Questions to Find Who You Are and What You Want In All Areas of Life,* then we'd appreciate that you leave a comment on Amazon! Reviews are the lifeblood of a publisher's work and we hope to count with yours! Also, to see more of our published titles go to http://bit.ly/GeraldConfienza

Thank you!

Gerald

Sources

https://tinybuddha.com/blog/recognizing-our-patterns-and-learning-how-to-change-them/

http://www.reflectionpond.com/blog/law-of-karma

https://www.psychologytoday.com/blog/changepower/201603/know-yourself-6-specific-ways-know-who-you-are

http://www.dadabhagwan.org/self-realization/

https://www.tonyrobbins.com/mind-meaning/why-you-are-the-way-you-are/

https://study.com/academy/lesson/self-understanding-and-self-concept.html

Find Your Passion

The Ultimate No-BS

Workbook

186 Questions, Prompts, and Exercises to Find

Your Passion, Work on Purpose, and Leave a

Lasting Legacy

GERALD CONFIENZA

Introduction

Is it real? Is it even possible?

We've all seen the YouTube videos and occasional Facebook ads with extremely successful people encouraging you to find your passion, monetize it, and live the dream life- only to sell us something in the end. Deep inside we all want a life lived at its maximum expression and in constant expansion. The great problem is that we don't know where to start. There was never a *How to Find Your Passion 101* class in college! Lack of self-knowledge and lack of clarity of what we should be doing is the great problem of our generation. If you're feeling lost too, then let me tell you something:

I've been there too.

A few years ago, I was in college studying for a degree I knew I was never going to use. I knew that there had to be a way in which I could use my talents to bring value to the world and create economic and holistic abundance in my life. However, whenever I tried to start anything, my undertakings would be short-lived. I tried to push myself through willpower alone, but, in the end, I'd always end up leaving projects half-done. My self-esteem plummeted as I grew increasingly disappointed in myself. I couldn't find that calling for which I was made and the idea of living the dream life was slowly drifting from sight.

I was blessed that during this time I met a friend named Sebastian Harth. More than a friend, he became an early mentor in my life and introduced me to the world of personal development. One of the ideas he reiterates in his mentorships is the importance of finding your passion and purpose through self-discovery. I took heed to his words and, thus, began in me a process of self-discovery and self-actualization. It's only been 4 years since then, but my life has completely changed. When I met Sebastian, I had barely enough money to eat- extreme, I know. But it's the truth. I had begun a business that I was injecting all my money into. My diet consisted of fruits and bread; that's how financially broke I was. Today, I am proud to be indefinitely retired from the workforce. I live off passive income, do what I love, and have absolute control of where I take my life from here on out.

Advice is a very cheap commodity that you shouldn't receive from just anyone. To illustrate this, during my seminars I always give the example of the college MBA professor who advises his or her students on how to start a business, when they've never started one themselves. How sound can advise derived only from theory be? I, instead, am somebody who is reaping the benefits of having worked insatiably on their passion for the last 4 years. From a place of coherence, I will guide you through a process that I have applied on myself and hundreds of others that will help you find your passion and instruct you into massive action.

In the pages that follow, I have compiled a series of carefully designed questions, prompts, and exercises laid out in workbook format. Completing these will instigate self-knowledge at a visceral level, probably like you've experienced before. I ask that you keep an open mind. Skepticism is ignorance's best friend. Only when we come with an empty cup can we get our cup filled. Answer these questions thoroughly and with no filter, and the workbook will reveal things about you that you didn't know yourself. I guarantee that, at the very least, you will find your passion. I say very least because my hope is that you also find your personal mission and life purpose.

This Workbook Belongs to…

An Integrated System: Laying Foundations

Here's a secret of overachievers: they have an *integrated system*. What's this system about?

A few years ago, I found myself talking with the leading authority in Neuro-linguistic Programming in the Hispanic world, Edmundo Velasco. I had ended up in one of his seminars through the recommendation of a friend. It was 8 hours of intense sessions and I was gladly receiving way more than my money's worth in information. For those who don't know, Edmundo was a business partner of John Grinder, the co-founder of Neuro-linguistic Programming (a.k.a. NLP), a science predominantly used in success coaching that studies human behavior in relation to neural maps.

Immediately after the seminar, I approached Dr. Velasco for some quick Q&A. The conversation ended with a few answers and a promise I'd sign up for his NLP course the following week. A great journey into the workings of the human mind had begun.

I had always wanted to know what makes great people great. The answer soon came. Edmundo was starting an introduction of Robert Dilt's Neurological Levels of the mind when he commented, "success and human achievement is very predictable. You see, extremely successful people have one thing in common: they have a powerful and, more importantly, integrated mindset. They have a set of empowering beliefs and values that are in harmony with their life purpose. There's no room for self-sabotage".

A light bulb flicked inside my head. That's it! That's what I was looking for!
I must've studied the material on developing an aligned, integrated mindset over a thousand times. I couldn't get enough.

As I continued my path in personal development and continued learning the workings of the human mind, I came across the same concept explained in diverse ways. Even World-class coach Tony Robbins teaches it in his seminars. I will explain it to you in the way that it was taught to me.

The Workings of the System

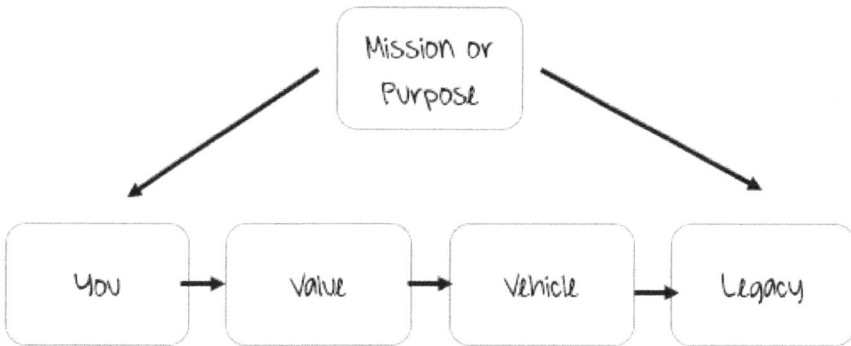

```
                    ┌─────────────┐
                    │  Mission or │
                    │   Purpose   │
                    └─────────────┘
              ↙                          ↘
┌─────────┐     ┌─────────┐     ┌─────────┐     ┌─────────┐
│   You   │ →   │  Value  │ →   │ Vehicle │ →   │ Legacy  │
└─────────┘     └─────────┘     └─────────┘     └─────────┘
```

The system above is made up of 5 different parts:

1. Finding your passion first begins with finding a mission or purpose that you feel a need to accomplish. Everyone has one. Yes, you do too and if you haven't found it already, we will do so on the following pages.
   Everyone has something they can't die without having done or contributed towards. E.g. lift people up, especially those who have been emotionally scarred during childhood.

2. After finding a worthwhile mission or purpose for ourselves, we must identify who we are. What makes you *you*? As mentioned, we're made up of beliefs and conditioning. The way we define ourselves will play a huge role in the way we're going to take action towards our mission.
   E.g. If you're a die-hard introvert and your mission is to lift people up, then instead of going in front of crowds of tens of thousands to reach out to your audience, you may prefer to use your writing as a means of communication.

3. The next step that will help narrow down possibilities even further is taking values into consideration. In order to make sure our emotional and moral needs are met through our actions, values have to be identified. If not, we could be working towards our mission yet still be miserable doing it. What's important to you? What do you value?

   E.g. If one of your predominant values is leaving your comfort zone, then despite being an introvert, you may still want to practice becoming a better public speaker and developing your own personal speaking style to get your message across. If, on the other hand, you value recognition the least and value sending a powerful message above anything, you may prefer to continue writing but under a pen name. For some people, the use of a pen name is indispensable if they want to bare themselves and their ideas to the world without inhibition.

4. Finally, we get to the part you've been looking for- the vehicle. The vehicle is the specific action in which you will hone your skill and through which you will accomplish your mission or purpose. The vehicle could be a specific, job, career, business idea, hobby, cause, etc. The vehicle is the means by which you will transmute your desire, your values, your identity, your sense of mission into concrete action that will lead to concrete results.

   E.g. Perhaps it's time to hone your skills in writing. Perhaps it's time to get a job in a large corporation that sells coaching and treatment for those with severe depression. Perhaps you want to open an NGO and blog about your coaching endeavors. You must choose one among the many vehicles available.

5. There, you've found your passion! You've taken all the elements that make up *you* and transformed them into an action through which you can take your life to its maximum expression. Are we done? Not yet. There's one, tiny, final, yet very crucial step. Legacy. Legacy defines the life of a human being. This brings back memories of me watching the Disney Movie *Coco* with my girlfriend. In this movie, the dead live on in the afterlife as long as they're still remembered for the things they did in life. Once everyone has forgotten who they are, they pass on to the unknown. I thought it was a tremendous analogy- to measure the value of one's life by the legacy they've left behind. Excuse me for going off on a tangent. Anyways, legacy is where we can check if our course of action is really what we want. Ask yourself, "What do you want to be remembered for?"
E.g. Perhaps for you it would be easier to find a job as a writer with work focused on helping others. However, you want to be remembered as someone more adventurous and entrepreneurial. Then, the logical choice would be to start your own business or NGO and focus on writing content that will add value to the life of thousands, if not millions.

Step 1: Finding Your Purpose

Easier said than done?

I think that's just an idea shared by people too lazy to look and search for information on their own. I don't think it's easy, but it's not hard either. Before we delve into finding your purpose, we'll clarify what purpose is not.

Your Purpose is Not...

Something you 'should' be doing. All our lives we've been told what to do and were forced into doing it whether we liked it or not. Remember that boring history class from 4th grade that had you grueling past the coursework the entire year? We've been conditioned to do things we don't want. We've also been conditioned to have decisions made for us. You know, the *go to school, get good grades, go to college, get a job, have kids, retire, and voila!* These are some of the key reasons as to why purpose is so elusive to many of us.

I'm not saying to *not* do any of the things mentioned above. I'm saying that you don't *have* to do them- it's not mandatory. Let me give you a hint: your purpose is never a *'should'* or a *'must'*. It's more of a *'want'*. This *'want'*, when fueled by decision and passion, eventually becomes a personal *'must'*. But, it always starts as a *'want'*. Martin Luther King Jr. was never obligated to fight for equal rights, he deeply wanted to. Actually, he was constantly told by his wife to stop, she knew what could happen if he continued. Despite his fear, Dr. King continued to live on purpose and eventually paid the ultimate price for the freedoms people of all races enjoy in the USA and around the world.

What Your Purpose Can Be
During a leadership summit, I heard the speaker say something that has stuck with me until today. "Life is God's gift to you. The way you live your life is your gift back to God". What a beautiful line. There's something I would add, though. It's not just the way you live your life, but the purpose you try to fulfill with it. *If you had to give up all your deeds in life as an offering to God (or to a force beyond yourself) and were evaluated by the positive change your deeds brought forth to creation (animals, people, planet, etc.), what would you want this change to be?*

What a Purpose-Filled Life Feels Like
Purpose is not a goal, it's the everyday living. Excuse the esoteric language, but I'm a firm believer that everything that happens to you in life happens for a reason. We've all heard this cliché, however, few of us actually question the events in our life (most just complain about them).

What am I supposed to learn from this? What is this event trying to show me about myself? How can I evolve from this event onwards? These are the right questions to ask. Why? Because when you take into account your personal story, your childhood, your parents, your personal traumas, the traumas you've seen others overcome, your imperfection, your weaknesses, your strengths, your skills, your talents, your desires, your longings, your role models, etc., then you begin to see a pattern. You begin to see a mission or purpose only someone who has lived your life and experienced everything you've experienced could do.

So, what does purpose feel like? It feels like *alignment*. It feels like congruence. It feels like wholeness. Above all there is certainty- that there's nothing else in the world you could be or should be doing other than *this*.

In the End, We Make Up Our Own Legend

Human beings are makers of history because we are makers of stories. Make up a story about yourself until it's one you feel congruent with. Until it's one that sums up everything that is *you*. That is what we will do with the following questions (and throughout the rest of the book). Enjoy the process!

Questions for Finding Your Purpose

In the following pages, you will encounter dozens of questions that will help you find your *purpose*. Answer them in detail and write as much as you can. Let your hand move on its own for once.

Finding Your Purpose: 57 Questions, Prompts, and Exercises

1. What would I change about the world, if I knew I could not fail?

2. At the end of my life, what would I most regret not having done?

3. If you knew that you will die 5 years from now, what would you spend your remaining life doing?

4. Describe a life that you would only have in nightmares. Sometimes knowing what we don't want helps us find what we want.

5. Why do I admire my role models?

6. Over the last month, when have you felt most motivated, inspired, and in a state of absolute focus? What were you doing? Who were you being?

7. What makes you happy? Yup, list everything.

8. If I could be granted the power to change the world, what would I do?

9. If my heart could talk, what would it say my purpose in life was?

10. What change brought forth to the lives of others by me would make me cry with joy, or brings tears to my eyes?

11. What is a horrible experience you would like to protect others from at all costs?

12. If my heart could talk, it would tell me to… (Hint: Describe actions you could take now)

13. What causes do you strongly believe in or connect with?

14. What perks up my curiosity?

15. What is something you've gone through and wish no one else ever had to? What is one thing someone should never have to experience?

16. What is the greatest and most memorable act of kindness a stranger has ever done for you? What would you say to that stranger?

17. Who in history would I most love to be, and why?

18. The world could change completely if people were to…

19. The greatest ideal people can dedicate their lives to is…

20. What would you tell your grandkids 50 years from now that you were the proudest of in your life?

21. As a kid, what are you about? Before any seriousness or ambition snuck in? Which memories most electrify your body/mind when you think of them?

22. What are the greatest problems you have encountered in your life? In overcoming them, what talents, gifts, and ideas have you developed?

23. How does you having lived on Earth and existed make humanity better?

24. What is the most important thing in my life?

25. If I had to make my best guess of my life's purpose, what would it be?

26. What would you like to have received help or mentorship with growing up? What was a hardship you wish someone would've helped you overcome?

27. What have I always been insecure about? What is one thing I could never overcome about myself?

28. What would you regret dying without having contributed towards?

29. What would I like to leave the world, as my legacy?

30. Over the last seven days, what moments have given you feelings of great love, deep satisfaction, or purpose?

31. What does triumph mean to you?

32. It's been over 100 years after your death. What impact your life has had on society is still felt today?

33. If I had to get started with something that would push me towards my life's purpose, what would it be?

34. What is one thing no one should die without having had experienced?

35. What do you want your epitaph to be?

36. Who are you most grateful for in your life? Make a list of those people and describe why.

37. What are you willing to pay the ultimate price for? What change would you like to see around you that you'd be willing to work day and night for?

38. What does legacy mean to you?

39. What qualities do my role models possess that I'd also like to be known for?

40. How would I define the life purpose of my role models?

41. You, your family, and your loved ones have all the time and money in the world. What would you dedicate your life to?

42. What challenge would I love to overcome, and then help others achieve the same?

43. Would 8-year-old you be proud of who you are today? What would he recommend that you do?

44. What do I most regret not doing, so far in my life?

45. What is the best way to help somebody else? Financially? Emotionally? Physically? Spiritually? Why?

46. What has been the greatest challenge that I have overcome so far in my life? Could I help other people to overcome that same challenge?

47. What special gift do I have that I could give to the world?

48. What do I want to insatiably learn about?

49. Who are the people I most admire for the legacy they've left behind?

50. What does *love* mean to you?

51. Perform a word-association exercise with the word purpose. When you're done, look over the list of words you've created. Is there a common theme? Or perhaps a mood? Freewrite for ten minutes regarding what you notice about your list.

52. Design a purpose-based vision board. In a wall or cardboard, pin down images and photos of what you want to see in your life. Make sure that what you're putting down is something that motivates you into action.

53. If you had to find images and photos that describe the contributions you would make to the world, what images would you collect? What images do you hold in your head and in your heart that sum up the life you want to live? How can you project the legacy you want to leave behind through these images? Make sure to add these images to the vision board assignment described above.

54. Ask your parents or a guardian who took care of you as a child. Ask them what cause 6-8yr old you would've loved to lead.

55. Find someone who you admire for the change he or she is making to his community, city, state, or country. Reach this person through phone or mail and ask him or her how they found their life purpose. Ask them to help you find yours.

56. Attend a leadership and legacy seminar or certification. This may imply a heavy cost but it's small compared to the value you'll get from it. Knowing your purpose in life has no value. The John Maxwell Team or any Anthony Robbins seminar are both great starting points.

57. Having completed all the previous questions, prompts, and exercises please narrow down your purpose to 5 purpose statements, by completing the affirmation: *My purpose in life is…* Having completed this, narrow your purpose further down to only one statement. It doesn't have to be perfect, it only has to feel right.

Step 2: Finding Yourself

Here's some short piece of wisdom everyone should incorporate into their lives by Socrates himself: *"Know thyself"*. I think we can all agree that all of wisdom and achievement begins first from knowing who you are at a visceral level.

Why?
Knowing who you are allows you to truly develop self-love and acceptance of who you are. Being able to see past your imperfections and embrace your strengths marks the beginning of self-esteem, and self-esteem is necessary for any great achievement. Look at a list of all of humanity's greatest achievers and you will find men and women with incredible self-esteem.

Salvador Dalí, easily the most prominent painter of the 20th century, was a Spanish surrealist with an uncanny sense of self-esteem. He was found routinely talking to himself in third person, addressing himself as you would address royalty. *"Does Master Dalí fancy some tea?"* He'd ask himself out loud when offered tea by hosts of parties and events. *"No, Master Dalí does not wish for tea"*, he'd reply. Yeah, pretty bizarre. He truly believed he was royalty, and that's probably why he painted like one.

If you know yourself, everything that makes you *you*, then decisions will come easily for you. Decisions are the shapers of your destiny. Recall a decision you made long ago that changed your entire life. Imagine what you'd be doing right now had you taken a different path. Actually, you need not go that far back. The decision to have purchased this workbook and the decision to complete it will set you off on a completely different path than if you had chosen to watch TV instead. See what I mean?

Who Am I?

Finding who you are, however, seems like no easy task. *Who am I?* is a question that has boggled the minds of the wisest men in history. As I'm clearly out of my league in making any contributions to this matter, I propose that we approach this topic from a psychological perspective and with a model that has shown results in the past. I'm referring to Robert Dilt's Logical Levels Model. Let me explain.

According to Robert Dilts, people's actions and results are made up of a logical mental model (or system) that's structured hierarchy. The more conscious, or aware, of we are of our psyche, the more superior logical levels we identify with. In short, when people are faced with the question, *who am I?* they will respond using any of the 7 subsets of logical levels you see in the image below.

Taken from http://www.management-learning.co.uk/single-post/2016/10/25/The-two-most-dangerous-words-for-managing-change

It's important to note from the image that a sense of purpose or mission that goes beyond ourselves (the one at the top) eventually defines the rest of what makes us who we are. This is why extremely successful people are more likely to define themselves by their mission rather than by their job position or their talents (and it's the first thing we did at the start of this workbook).

Why is This Important?
Knowing where we fit in the lower levels can allow us to use our strengths to our advantage when working towards our purpose, and/or help us change and adapt to varying beliefs, values or behaviors, if necessary. This is of crucial importance because many times we narrow down *'our passion'* to a simple skill or capability. This is a terrible mistake. The truth is that it's a bit more complicated.

We may be skilled at playing, *e.g.*, tennis, and may find success in this sport, however, if our values, sense of identity, and purpose are not aligned with this activity, then we'll never find any lasting fulfillment in its practice. The opposite is true as well. We may have no particular talent for the sport, but if we have a *burning desire* (purpose) to, *e.g.*, help people develop confidence in themselves, *identify* ourselves as givers of empowerment, and *believe* we can achieve anything we put our mind to, then, even if we lack the talent, we can *learn* professional tennis and use our success as a means of inspiration for the masses. In the latter case, we have identified where we fit in highest logical levels and this knowledge has pushed us into developing a skill to a professional level.

Stop Defining Your Passion Solely as An Activity, It's Much More Than That

Let me elaborate. Many people believe they have no talents at all and therefore stop their search for their passion. If you're one of those, then let me tell you something: it doesn't matter at all you have tons of talents or have none. Yup, you read me right. What matters is *why* and *for what purpose* you'd be willing to learn new skills or talents. *Purpose is the catalyst of all great achievements.*

Questions to Find Yourself

Well, it's time for you to find *you!* Join me for the following questions, prompts and exercises to identify *who you are* at each of the logical levels. As in the first section of the book we already covered purpose-based questions, questions here will focus on the lower levels: identity, beliefs/values, capabilities, behaviors and environmental.

Finding Who You are: 100 Questions, Prompts, and Exercises

Environment Level

Humans are creatures made to adapt to their environment. Our environment, whether we like it or not, shapes us in certain ways. Therefore, our first step in getting to know ourselves is identifying *how* our environment is dictating the way we behave and think. In this section, we will focus mostly on evaluating our inner circle of influence, perhaps one of the most important external factors that can make or break us.

1. Where do you spend the most time\Where do you like to spend the most time? Why?

2. Where would you like to spend the most time? Why?

3. Where wouldn't you like to spend any time at all? Why not?

4. Where do you your friends and family fit in your life? Do you prefer spending time with either group over the other? Why?

5. I love to spend time with people who...

6. What kind of people do you surround yourself with?

7. Why do you spend time with them?

8. Do you think that the people you spend the most time with at the moment add value to your life? Or do they take away from you?

9. Late success psychology expert Jim Rhon once said, "*you are the average of the 5 people you spend the most time with*". Make a list of the 5 people you spend the most time with. Next to their names, add in adjectives and values that they hold and embody. Do these describe you as well? Next, pick out these adjectives and values and hand them to somebody you know. Ask them if these values and adjectives describe *you*. What's their opinion?

10. Having completed the exercise above, do you agree or disagree with Jim Rhon?

11. Having concluded the exercise above, we will proceed to do the same but under different criteria. Evaluate each one of the five people you spend the most time in a scale from 1-10 in the area of relationships, personal finances, spirituality, health, and results in life (results related to their own purpose). Next, do the same with you. Do you see any similarities?

12. Would you change the people that you spend the most time with? Or are you happy with the results? This question is necessary as the most common problem people face when starting anything new is resistance from their inner circle. Most people have never evaluated their inner circle before and have inadvertently let in toxic individuals into their life. Thus, it's quite common to find individuals with dreams and ambitions who are left paralyzed by the discouragement of those closest to them.

13. If it's necessary to change your inner circle, please list the predominant qualities you'd love for your inner circle to have.

Behavioural Level

Now it's time to look at the way we behave and our reactions to external stimuli. By understanding our behaviour, we can begin to analyse areas of strength and areas in need of improvement. Remember that anything at this level in the logical level pyramid can be easily changed. Don't be afraid to be honest with your answers to the following questions.

Adaptability

14. How do you handle difficult situations?

15. What do you do when your priorities change quickly? Describe a situation when this occurred and detail your reaction?

16. What your first reaction when you lose control of something that matters to you?

Ambition

17. How have you demonstrated your willingness to work hard in your previous endeavors? If not, what would you say the reason was?

18. What were (are) your study patterns in school? Describe a time when you work relentlessly to achieve an objective.

19. What project, job, or undertaking are you proud of having completed? What did it consist of? How hard did you work to achieve it?

20. Do you prefer getting things done without supervision? Why or why not?

21. Do you work harder with or without supervision? Why or why not?

22. What is the biggest risk you've taken in the past when following your gut? Detail your undertaking.

23. Describe an ideal challenge you'd like to take on?

Analytical Thinking

24. Are details more your thing? Or do you prefer focusing on broad, big-picture objectives?

25. Recall a time where you had to work on details to get the job done. How did you feel about working on details? Is it something you'd like to de again?

26. Imagine you're the CEO of a large corporation. Would you be strict on following procedure? Or would you prefer to give employees more freedom in decision-making according to personal discretion? What does this say about your behavior in social groups?

27. Do you prefer to act leveraging powerful emotions in your favor? Or do you prefer to act after analyzing all possible solutions? What does this tell you about your decision-making process?

Relationships

28. Recall a time you had to deal with someone who was extremely angry at you. How were you able to communicate with them? Were you able to get your message across?

29. Are you likely to make more friends out of people you approached or are all friends of yours part of your extended inner circle?

30. What do you do when you want to genuinely connect with others?

31. What about when you want to connect them to your cause? Is there any way this could be improved?

32. Teamwork, in my opinion, is…

33. Leadership, in my opinion, is…

34. How do you act when your part of a group as opposed to when you're on your own? Which do you prefer?

Getting Results

35. Do you engage in goal-setting? Why or why not?

36. What would your choice of motivation be, if you had to create an incentive for your team to perform?

37. Describe the steps someone has to take to overcome challenges in their life.

38. Do you prefer to work to please those around you or would you rather do something for the good of everyone around you even if it gets you on their bad side?

39. What are you more likely to do, plan every detail of a project before taking action, or take action even if you only have a minimum amount of information? How is this pattern of behavior dictating the results you currently have? Is there any correlation? Why or why not?

Efficiency and Discipline

40. How do you get around doing things that are not mandatory?

41. Do you prefer working harder or working smarter? How could you combine both to achieve bigger results?

42. When you say you're busy, is it because you're focusing on things that are important or urgent? Note that, *e.g.*, going to a routine medical checkup could be *urgent* (if it's already on your agenda for the day), but reading a book or meeting up with mentors that could help you get started on your purpose could be far more *important* for your life.

43. Are the things that you're doing on a daily basis getting you closer to your end goal? If not, how can you fix it?

44. In a scale from 1-10, how much do your emotions get in the way of you getting things done? How can we begin to use our emotions as leverage to get more done instead?

Communication

45. Are you more likely to listen or talk during one on one conversations?

46. How comfortable do you feel communicating unpleasant things to others or superiors?

47. Describe how you would get a group of people to join your cause.

48. In an argument, are you more willing to compromise or do you choose to impose your point of view to the very end?

49. Ever had difficulty speaking up? Describe a situation that left you nervous to speak up. Why did you feel this way?

50. How willing are you to take accountability and say *'I'm sorry'*?

51. How good do you consider yourself building rapport with others?

Skills and Capabilities Level

In finding your purpose in life, knowing what skills and capabilities you're already equipped with is of tremendous importance. In the following questions, we will narrow down your talents and skills and identify areas of expertise you may want to develop.

What have you always wanted to get good at? Great talent is not always something you're born with, most times it's something you develop.

52. Make a list of 25 things you think you're good at.

53. Make a list of 25 things that you like doing the most (except things like *eating* or *sleeping*).

54. What's a common denominator in the jobs, classes or assignments you've had in the past that you love?

55. What activities make you lose track of time (again, no sleeping, no scrolling past newsfeeds, etc)?

56. What activities did you indulge in as a kid? What kept you so engaged in them?

57. Grab your mom or guardian who raised you as a child. What did they think you'd end up growing up to be? What talents did they identify in you from a young age?

58. What did you love to do as a teen?

59. According to you, what are your greatest strengths?

60. According to a close family member, what are your greatest strengths?

61. According to a colleague or professor, what are your greatest strengths?

62. What topic or skill do others ask for your help in?

63. Make a list of activities that make you feel energized.

64. What topic sparks up your curiosity and makes you want to learn more about it?

65. What would you learn insatiably about?

66. What activities get you in a state of *flow*?

67. If you were to wake up tomorrow feeling free and excited about the upcoming day, what activities would this day be full of?

68. Intrinsically, do you feel that you were born to do any one thing?

69. What would you even if you weren't paid to do it?

Values and Beliefs Level

In this section, we will identify values and beliefs that have shaped the way you have lived life until now. In the questions that follow, we will also adjust the beliefs and values we have so that we may achieve more. We will start with values and continue with beliefs.

Values: The following exercise is taken directly from *Mindtools.com*. Please visit the following link on their site for the full article: http://bit.ly/FindingValues. Gauging what's important to you is of utmost importance for finding the way you'll choose to express your purpose. Values define you and are the base for the decisions you will make in your life. The way you will find expression of your identity and fulfill your purpose is extremely dependent on your core values. Take your time answering the following questions.

Part 1- Identifying Times When You Were Happy: Try to base your answers both on your personal and professional life.

70. What were you doing?

71. Were you with other people? Who?

72. What other factors contributed to your happiness?

Step 2: Identify the times when you the proudest: Base your answers both on your personal and professional life.

73. What other factors contributed to your happiness?

74. Why were you proud?

75. Did other people share your pride? Who?

76. What other factors contributed to your feelings of pride?

Step 3: Identify the times when you were most fulfilled and satisfied:
Base your answers on your personal and professional life.
77. What need or desire was fulfilled?

78. How and why did the experience give your life meaning?

79. What other factors contributed to your feelings of fulfillment?

Step 4: Determine your top values: Base this on your experiences of happiness, pride, and fulfillment. This is easily one of the most important exercises for self-discovery you'll probably ever do. From the following list of values, pick only ten.

Acceptance	Control
Achievement	Conviction
Accountability	Cooperation
Adaptability	Courage
Alertness	Courtesy
Altruism	Creation
Ambition	Creativity
Amusement	Credibility
Assertiveness	Curiosity
Attentive	Decisiveness
Awareness	Dedication
Balance	Dependability
Beauty	Determination
Boldness	Devotion
Bravery	Dignity
Brilliance	Discipline
Calm	Discovery
Certainty	Drive
Challenge	Effectiveness
Charity	Efficiency
Cleanliness	Empathy
Clever	Empower
Commitment	Endurance
Communication	Energy
Community	Enjoyment
Compassion	Enthusiasm
Competence	Equality
Concentration	Ethical
Confidence	Excellence
Connection	Experience
Consciousness	Exploration
Contentment	Expressive
Contribution	

Fairness	Lawful
Family	Leadership
Famous	Learning
Fearless	Liberty
Feelings	Logic
Focus	Love
Freedom	Loyalty
Friendship	Mastery
Fun	Maturity
Generosity	Meaning
Genius	Moderation
Giving	Motivation
Goodness	Openness
Grace	Optimism
Gratitude	Order
Greatness	Organization
Growth	Originality
Happiness	Passion
Hard work	Patience
Harmony	Peace
Health	Persistence
Honesty	Playfulness
Honor	Potential
Hope	Power
Humility	Productivity
Imagination	Professionalism
Improvement	Prosperity
Independence	Purpose
Individuality	Quality
Innovation	Realistic
Inspiring	Recognition
Integrity	Recreation
Intelligence	Reflective
Intensity	Respect
Intuitive	Responsibility
Irreverent	Restraint
Joy	Results-oriented
Justice	Reverence
Kindness	Rigor
Knowledge	Risk

Satisfaction	Sustainability
Security	Talent
Self-reliance	Teamwork
Selfless	Thoughtful
Service	Timeliness
Sharing	Tolerance
Significance	Toughness
Silence	Traditional
Simplicity	Tranquility
Sincerity	Trust
Skill	Truth
Smart	Understanding
Solitude	Unity
Spirituality	Valor
Spontaneous	Victory
Stability	Vigor
Status	Vision
Stewardship	Vitality
Strength	Wealth
Structure	Winning
Success	Wisdom
Support	Wonder
Surprise	

80. Make a list of the 10 values that most resonate with you in this list.

81. Rank the 10 values in order from least important to you, to most important. The value ranked at the top is your essence.

Step 6: Reaffirm your values. Check your top-priority values, and make sure that they fit with your life and your vision for yourself.

82. Do these values make you feel good about yourself?

83. Are you proud of your top three values?

84. Would you be comfortable and proud to tell your values to people you respect and admire?

85. Do these values represent things you would support, even if your choice isn't popular, and it puts you in the minority?

Beliefs: Beliefs dictate a lot about our lives. Ever had the problem of not being able to get yourself to do something? Or finally doing it and end up sabotaging yourself? The greatest asset in our power as humans is our belief system. However, they can also be our greatest liability if left unattended. In this section, we will identify our empowering beliefs and limiting beliefs and begin a process of change.

86. What 3 negative thoughts/beliefs do you have that set you back the most?

87. Why do you have those beliefs? Make your answer as long as it needs to be. Take your time as you probe around for answers.

88. Rate each limiting belief from 1 to 10, with one being the least limiting and 10 being the most limiting. Which of your beliefs is the one that limits you the most? Why?

89. How have these limiting belief drained you in life? How have they held you back? Describe the pain having these beliefs has caused you.

90. If you let go of these limiting belief, what would happen? How would it transform your life? Please detail changes in your life that would happen individually for each of the 3 beliefs.

91. What's the worst that can happen if you were to act despite your limiting beliefs? Is it as bad as you've made seen in your brain? Do this exercise for all three limiting beliefs.

92. Each of the three limiting beliefs is stopping you from high achievement in their respective areas of your life. If you didn't have these limiting beliefs, what goals would you set for yourself in these areas of your life? How high would you aim?

93. Detail circumstances in which each of the limiting beliefs you've mentioned have been proved wrong. *E.g.,* if your limiting belief is that it takes money to make money, then can you come up with an example of a millionaire who started out in absolute poverty?

94. If you were to put your limiting belief on *hold* for a week (imagine it didn't exist) and chose to act is if you didn't have it, what would you do? Do this exercise for all three limiting beliefs?

95. Assign an area of your life to where each of these limiting beliefs reside (e.g. *'I am not good looking'* could be assigned under *Love $ Relationships*). Now, set for yourself a challenging goal in this area of your life. Remember that we're putting our limiting beliefs *on hold*, so it's okay to act as if you didn't have them. What 3 baby steps can you start taking right now to make that goal a reality?

96. This one may take a while, but I promise you that your life will be thoroughly enriched from completing the following exercise. I want you to take the remaining space on the page and divide it into 5 parts (like a pie chart). Each slice of the pie will represent one area of your life: Love (relationships, including family and friends), Wealth, Health, Results (Personal Achievement), Spirituality. In each one of these areas, write down 3 limiting beliefs that have held you back.

97. As a follow up to the previous exercise, please design a similar pie chart with the five areas of your life. Now, instead of writing down 3 limiting beliefs, write down 3 empowering beliefs you'd like to adopt in each of these areas.

Identity Level

Identity: This one's a tough one. At an identity level, we are the sum of the answers you've written thus far and much, much, more. Though few people hardly change at this level throughout their lives, it's quite possible to do it. I've encountered many people that, though they grew up in a horrible environment and adopted numerous limiting beliefs growing up (such as *'I'm worthless'*), desperately saw to change that and began working on their mind. If you asked them who they are today, they'd say something along the lines of *'I'm an ordinary human being with an extraordinary sense of purpose'*. My friend Henry is such case. He grew up in very poor living conditions and with little self-esteem. One day his life changed when he met a successful individual who lent him a hand, gifted him a book, and encouraged him to believe in himself. Henry developed the insatiable desire to become like this man. Today, Henry travels the world, is financially free, has more friends than he could count, and has become his family's pride and joy.

Henry's example has taught me that you should not define yourself only by who you are at this moment, but also by what you want to become. In the end, humans are the architects of their destiny. Therefore, I have only two prompts in this section: the former will get you writing about who you are right now, and the latter will get you writing about who you desperately want to become.

98. Who is (insert your name here)? In third person (using he/she, not me/I), write who (insert your name here) is. What is he or she about? What's their essence like? Spend the rest of the page writing about this very important person.

99. Now, final question. Who or what does (insert your name here) want to become? What's his or her ideal self? Spend the rest of the page detailing the future (insert your name here).

Purpose Level

Purpose: It all goes back to this: the purpose to which we'll dedicate our lives to fulfill. Luckily for us, we've already completed this part at the beginning of the workbook. If for some reason you haven't already, smack yourself in the head and go back to square one.

Step 3: What Do You Value?

We've identified our purpose, we know who we are, now it's just time to find our values. For this, please refer back to questions 71 through 86 *Self Discovery @ the Values and Beliefs Level*. By questions 86, you should've already found the values that most resonate with you, ranked the top 10 from least important to most important, and have identified your #1 value. Are you in agreement with what you found? What could be modified?

Make sure to have these fresh in your mind as they will be crucially important for the next step in this process of finding your passion- *choosing the right vehicle*.

Step 4: Choosing Your Vehicle

When people start their search for their passion, this is the level at which most stay. This is why people have such a tough problem deciding what to do in life. They're trying to choose a job, career, or business that is right for them, without having first considered what *'right'* is and who *they* really are.

Well, first things first. What's a vehicle? *A vehicle is a means by which you can reach your purpose, through the expression your identity, staying within the boundaries of your values, and making full use of your skills and capabilities.* It's what people will actually see you doing.

Finding Your Vehicle: 26 Questions, Prompts, and Exercises

Climbing the Career Ladder vs Diving into Entrepreneurship

The first thing we must do is find if you have entrepreneurial qualities in you. Being your own boss is becoming more and more accessible due to opportunities found on the internet, MLM companies, and even in the traditional business world. Your true calling may be found here. If it's not, however, rest at ease. Many people would rather avoid the unnecessary risk and grind of the entrepreneurial world and, instead, focus on perfecting their craft. That's valid as well.

In this section, we will identify the vehicle you will use to fulfill your purpose. First, we will evaluate if you have entrepreneurial tendencies through the *Entrepreneur Test*. Afterward, we will guide you through a list of questions to determine the vehicle (in the entrepreneur world or the career world) that will be most suitable for you.

Entrepreneur Test

1. Are you willing to pay the price? Entrepreneurship comes at a huge cost (not just monetary!), that you must pay out before seeing any results. This includes hardly getting in any sleep for a while, having people not believe in you, having others saying you're crazy and having you doubt yourself constantly.

2. Are you willing to start a process of never-ending learning and growth? Though this is true for any person living out their purpose, it's especially true for entrepreneurs because they will have to find mentors and adopt new habits early on if they want to see any progress.

3. Do you prefer to be a loner, or do you prefer working in groups? John C. Maxwell says that *"One is too small a number to achieve greatness"*. Entrepreneurs must be willing to recruit others into their business and be able to delegate work to leverage their actions. If you prefer working on your own, entrepreneurship may not be for you.

4. Do you like to sell? Or does the mere thought of it make you cringe? Every business must sell to survive. If leadership is the top quality that makes or breaks entrepreneurs, then selling is a close second. That brings me to the next question...

5. Are you a leader? Or are you willing to develop leadership qualities? Great businessmen are great leaders. Leadership is influence, nothing more and nothing less. The ability to influence your partners, your stakeholders, your workers, your clients, etc., is indispensable if you want to achieve great things with your venture. Growing your leadership is a life-long process, but it takes around 3-5 years to develop the leadership skills necessary to sustain a growing business.

6. How good are you at meeting new people? If not good at all, are you willing to commit to mastering this skill? Business is all about people. Your ability to meet new business partners, mentors, clients, etc., will play an important role in expanding your reach.

7. How well do you adapt to ever-changing scenarios? Business is evolving rapidly, at a rate that has never been seen in history. A quick look at industry disruptors such as Uber, Amazon, Air BnB, etc., can verify this. A great businessman must understand what Charles Darwin understood a few hundred years ago: *"It's not the strongest species that survives, it's the quickest to adapt to changes in its environment"*.

8. How demanding are you of the people you let into your life? I don't mean this in the negative sense either. But it's necessary that those who you let into your inner circle add value to your life. If there are any toxic people in your inner circle, they will subtract energy from you. Contradicting emotions, unnecessary drama, and toxicity are the last things entrepreneurs need in order to move forward.

9. Which do you value more: security or achievement? Business is incredibly volatile and uncertain during its period of infancy. There will be times in which you may make a lot of money right away, and there will be times where you won't even be able to pay yourself. Your drive to succeed must stronger than your need for security, especially at the beginning.

10. Do you have the humility to ask for help? Or do you think you can do it all on your own? This goes back to Maxwell's saying about needing others to achieve great things. However, you must not only be a team player, you must also know when to admit you're wrong and go to others to ask for help. In whatever undertaking, there's always someone who has already gone to the top. We can save ourselves months or years of trial and error by getting help from those who've already achieved it.

11. How badly do you want it? How ecstatic do you get from visualizing your business succeed? What causes will your business represent? How intense is your desire? The greatest common denominator of all business success is *burning desire*. You have to have it.

Evaluation: If you've answered *yes* to at least 8 of the 11 questions then you've got entrepreneur material in you. I suggest that you look into entrepreneurship as a real possibility for you and start evaluating the kind of project you'd like to create. It doesn't even have to be a for-profit-business; it could be an NGO you're after. Don't have the money? Then, I'd suggest starting a part-time business while keeping your full-time job. Once you're making more money from your business, then you can quit your job. That's what I did!

Disclaimer & What this evaluation is not: Just because you didn't answer '*yes*' to all of these doesn't mean you're not cut out to be an entrepreneur. I was a want-trepreneur at age 17. At that age, I had a lot of ego (with no real basis for it), wouldn't ask others for help, was a huge loner, hated meeting people, and valued security over success. And it was true- at that age, I wasn't really ready for what I was getting into. My first relative success with business came at age 20 when I finally started making money (profit!) from a business idea I had launched. While I didn't have the skillset, I did have desire and persistence. It's these two traits that kept me going despite the setbacks and discouragement I received from friends and family. Therefore, this evaluation is not the be all, end all evaluation- I don't think there will ever be one. All that's necessary to be successful in the long-term in entrepreneurship is burning desire and persistence, as these two traits will bring about all others in due time. What this evaluation is: a measure by which to gauge if you're ready to start a business *now, at this moment.*

For Entrepreneurs!

You've decided it! Entrepreneurship is for you, and you're not going to let anything stop you. Perfect! In the following questions, we will ask you to analyze possible ventures an ideas that will take into account all the things we've covered thus far. Note that this is also applicable if you're trying to start a non-profit.

12. Taking into consideration what we've talked about purpose, identity (including skills and capabilities), and values, make a list of all the possible business ideas that you'd like to develop that would be in alignment with each one of these aspects about yourself. Take your time with this list, you're welcome to make it as long as possible.

13. Hope you have a lot of ideas written down. Narrow down this list by making your top ten favorite business ideas.

14. Next to each business idea, describe *why* you'd be willing to start it. Is your *why* compelling enough?

15. Next to each business idea, describe the *value* you'd be giving your clients (or the problem you're trying to solve for them). Does solving this particular problem resonate with you?

16. Next to each business idea, describe the *reward* you'd get from starting and growing it. Does the *reward* excite you?

17. Next to each business idea, describe why people should choose *you* above all other competitors? What makes *you* stand out?

Having answered all of these questions will narrow the list down to only a few candidates. The only three remaining factors to analyze are the market, resources, and your ability to leverage your efforts.

18. To evaluate the market ask yourself: Is there a real demand for what I'm doing? How easily can I enter the market?

19. As for resources: what resources would you need to start this project? If you don't have them all, what's the minimum required to just *start*?

20. As for leverage: is your project scalable? What actions can you take now (and during the process of starting your business) that will have the most effect on it long term?

21. Finally, what business path have you chosen?

For Professionals!

None of that entrepreneurial nonsense- you're more the kind who wants to craft their skill and take it to the highest level. Great stuff. To narrow down the vehicle you use to fulfill your purpose, answer the following questions.

22. Taking into account your purpose, identity, and values, what skill or ability that you can put into the service of others do you want to commit to mastering? Make a list of at least 5 of these.

23. Next to each of the skills or abilities, detail who you'd want to do them for. *E.g. NGOs, large corporations, individuals, agencies, political groups, etc.* Choose one entity that resonates with you.

24. Next to each of the skills or abilities, detail the need or the want you will satisfy of the client/organization/individual you mentioned above.

25. Ask yourself: how does this entity change as a result? Does being responsible for this change excite me?

26. After having examined and evaluated your top five skills and abilities, complete the following writing prompt. *The vehicle I have chosen to fulfill my purpose is…*

Step 5: The Making of a Legacy

The secret to living an extraordinary life: to actively craft the legacy you want to leave behind through your actions. My mentor used to say, *"Most people's lives revolve around eating, shi**ing, and sleeping. It's no wonder that no one remembers them after they die"*. It's raw, a bit offensive, but ultimately true. Only the people who actively crafted their legacy in life can be remembered. We all hold a belief that our life must have some kind of meaning. If not, it wouldn't be worth living. Through the years, I have learned that there's no better person to designate this meaning other than yourself.

- *But Gerald, haven't we covered the questions about legacy already?*
- *Yes.*

But, you see, it's also the question that we finish this process of self-discovery with. Once you've found your designated vehicle, you must ask whether it really is the best option through which you'll fulfill your life's purpose.

1. Can this vehicle set me off on the right path towards accomplishing my life's purpose?

2. Would you be proud of the legacy you'd leave behind if you chose this vehicle as your only means towards fulfilling your mission?

3. Note that the vehicle you use to fulfill your purpose can change at different stages of your life. What's important is if the vehicle you're choosing is correct for you *now*. Is this the correct vehicle for fulfilling my life's purpose *at this very moment?*

Conclusion: The Secret Step to Living with Passion

Congrats for making it this far! Now comes the important part: *Action.*

Action is the most key component to living with passion. There could be an activity that is in alignment with your purpose, identity, and values, however, if you're not putting in the effort to master your craft, then it will never develop into a passion. I'll let you in on a little secret- it's repetition, focus, and massive action that turns an activity into a passion, not the other way around. So, don't wait, don't procrastinate, and decide to take action immediately on the discoveries you've made by completing this workbook.

How I Discovered My Passion

All my life growing up, I suffered from poor self-esteem and had a very pessimistic outlook on what would become my future. Very deep down, though, I knew I wanted to be of positive impact on the lives of others. Opportunity came knocking on my door a few days after my 18th birthday. I was presented with a network marketing business opportunity and saw the possibility of making some much-needed extra cash on the side. I accepted right away as I was barely making ends meet as a college sophomore. I decided to become coachable and learn from the person who sponsored me and from the company's educational system. What happened later became a nearly life-changing experience for me. I began listening to audios of successful people, started reading books about successful people, and assisting conferences where successful people gathered. This was a kind of association that I had never experienced before in my life. Soon, the way I thought and acted changed. I began seeing a puzzle unfold before my eyes.

At first, I only did network marketing for the money. I saw young people my age who were financially free and never had to work again. I desperately wanted a life like theirs. However, as I grew in rank and team volume, I began seeing my daily network marketing activities as a powerful vehicle for achieving my purpose. For as long as I can remember I've always wanted to inspire others to believe more in themselves. This is, in part, because I wish I could've had someone to serve as my inspiration during my teenage years. With every new recruit that joined my business, I saw myself playing the role of a mentor and leader. I had to create a genuine friendship with each one of them, empower them, and teach them through example how the business worked. Some people entered the business with ridiculously low self-esteem, others with ridiculously high egos. Nevertheless, it was my job the guide them and forge leadership qualities in each one of them.

Network marketing soon became a vehicle that was in alignment with my purpose, values, beliefs- and eventually, my skills and talents. Starting out, I had zero leadership qualities, I stuttered when speaking in front of a crowd, and I lacked basic communication skills. However, because the idea of helping others to believe in themselves (specifically in their ability to lead masses and create financial freedom) was so *exciting* for me, I learned to develop these skills. It didn't take long for me to find myself standing in crowds of thousands of people sharing my story.

Before *discovering* my passion, I was aware very aware of the network marketing business model but had never paid much attention to it. I knew you had to create a team of consumers and distributors and that you could generate passive income from their consumption or sales- it just didn't seem appealing to me at all. Without having *put in the necessary action* I would've never discovered that this was my passion. Always remember that *action begets passion*, not the other way around.

Having said that there are two possible scenarios that may have resulted from you finding your vehicle through this workbook. First, your vehicle may be something that you anticipated, and thus you may have found yourself in familiar territory. If that's the case, passion may be easier to develop. If, however, the vehicle you've found is something you didn't expect, then don't knock it until you try it. Be willing to give it chance. Try, experiment, live. There is no right or wrong, there is no time limit. I always push my friends, business partners, and downlines to do everything in urgency, but never in a rush- there's a difference. Take action with abandon, with urgency. But, also know deep down that it's okay to make mistakes. So, go ahead, begin planning your next move. This may very well be the start of the legacy you'll leave behind.

References

- Vance, Ashlee. Elon Musk: Tesla, SpaceX, And The Quest For A Fantastic Future. : . Print.
- Maxwell, John C. The 17 Indisputable Laws of Teamwork: Embrace Them and Empower Your Team. Nashville: T. Nelson, 2001. Print.
- Aileron. "The Only Entrepreneur Test You Will Ever Need." Forbes, Forbes Magazine, 4 June 2012, www.forbes.com/sites/aileron/2012/06/04/the-only-entrepreneur-test-you-will-ever-need/#358d001a3af7.
- Davenport, Barrie. "15 Probing Questions to Help You Bust Through Limiting Beliefs." Expert Enough, expertenough.com/2959/15-probing-questions-to-help-you-bust-through-limiting-beliefs.
- "What Are Your Values?: Deciding What's Most Important in Life." From MindTools.com, www.mindtools.com/pages/article/newTED_85.htm.
- "How to Discover Your Mission, Values, Purpose and Legacy." Asian Efficiency, 13 Aug. 2015, www.asianefficiency.com/systems/discover-mission-values-purpose-legacy/.
- "15 Questions That Reveal Your Ultimate Purpose in Life." Goodlife Zen, 16 Mar. 2018, goodlifezen.com/15-questions-that-reveal-your-ultimate-purpose-in-life/.

Coaching Questions:

200 Breakthrough Questions for Career and Business Mastery

GERALD CONFIENZA

Coaching Yourself with Self-Questioning: Introduction

Back in the days when I was still in the telecom industry, I met someone – an enthusiastic, dream-filled man in his early 30s. Let's call him Jack. We may not have had the luxury of time to hang out outside of work, but we regularly caught up whenever we had the chance- usually during lunch breaks. He was an admirable family man. He was the kind of husband who'd spend his days off lending his wife a hand; the kind of father who'd take initiative to play with his 3-year-old son, the kind of guy who'd always decline our colleagues' invitations to hang out during weekends. I had been working there a few months when he came, and his occasional queries about reports paved the way for our budding friendship. Everything was a smooth sailing for us and the rest of our team. That all changed when upper management decided to transfer him to another department.

In just a few months, I saw his drastic transition from a cheerful go-getter to someone who rarely smiled at the office. I heard the financial department was a stressful place to be in, but I didn't realize how serious it was until I saw him in that state. When I finally had the chance to speak with him, he vented out how mentally and physically draining his new tasks were, not to mention he had a few work-related issues with some colleagues. At times, despite not being able to get enough rest, he was even worried to call in sick because he just didn't want to be confronted by his very strict supervisor. I advised him to file a short vacation leave just to loosen up, you know, set priorities straight. The way I saw it, he had them all tangled up. It would a short leave to reward himself for everything he had to endure on a daily basis. He tapped me on the shoulders, smiled, and said: *"Man, I couldn't afford to take one."* All he wanted was to provide a permanent home for his family and finally stop spending on monthly rentals. So despite the hefty workload and stressful environment, he continued working and promised to stop only when he had enough savings to pay for that small condominium unit he'd been eyeing.

A couple more months have passed, and his health started to decline. Too much exhaustion caused him some physical discomfort, in addition to his unstable blood pressure. I did my best to talk him out of that unhealthy work routine, to no avail. He wanted to earn more but totally forgot to invest in good health which is an essential factor for anyone's success. As a friend, I wanted him to realize that our savings would be useless if, at the end of the day, we're just going to spend it on sustaining our medications, all because we took our health for granted.

But as much as I wanted to continue monitoring his situation, some personal stuff came up and I needed to pursue other things. I left the company, hoping to one day catch up with my previous workmates, especially Jack. My friend clearly had a good intention, but it didn't necessarily lead him to good results, which sometimes made me wonder, *"Where did Jack go wrong?"*

He focused on his goals to the point that he became oblivious to his own needs, both physiological and emotional. His judgment was clouded with the unbalanced desire to be successful. *He had clear goals but had lost sight of the larger picture.* Why? A great navigator must triumph over the daily problems that may affect a ship. However, no matter how arduous these become, a navigator must never lose sight of the destination. The destination for Jack may have been buying a condo, but what did that condo really represent? It represented a home, a place where he and his family could enjoy and feel the security of a having a place that's truly theirs. However, if the provider, in this case, Jack, falls ill, sacrifices his emotional and psychological well-being in the process, and becomes unable to keep providing for his family, then what? Then all of Jack's efforts become in vain. *All because Jack never took the time to stop, breathe and ask himself the right questions.*

I wrote this book as an invitation for my dear readers to do just that. As we progress in anything, it inevitably becomes routine. When we're in a routine, our minds become fixed and we tend to think there's only one way to reach a certain outcome.

Think about it.

I'm sure we could all agree that, had Jack taken the time to sit down and think about other ways of getting what he wanted, he could've come up with something. Jack could've easily asked for his old position back and have started a side business to make up for the income reduction. He could've started an online business as a side project. He could've negotiated fewer hours. He could've been honest to his superiors about his declining health and motivation. He could've looked for another job. The point is, the world is not black and white, nor is the acquisition of our life's objectives fixed in only one possible path.

It's because of this that I have designed this book to be an interactive, almost journal-like, series of questions to encourage self-discovery in one of the most important areas of our lives which is our occupation. Self-awareness is a powerful tool we need to acquire and it's something you can start incorporating into your life with just one question a day. Experts agree that coaching yourself through questions is a powerful tool to self-discovery. World-renowned coach Anthony Robbins always tells us in his seminars that the quality of our lives depends on the quality of the questions we ask ourselves. He's not wrong. And so, I encourage you to go through these questions (or study them so you can have others go through them), let go of any filters and respond with full honesty. Like a journal, answer one or two questions a day.

"Your choices decide your fate. Take the time to make the right ones."
- Unknown

Benefits of Self-Awareness

Aristotle once said, "knowing yourself is the beginning of all wisdom". This statement hits it right on the mark. Due to the educational system we grew up in, we were fed ideas about success that aren't necessarily true anymore. The idea of graduating college, getting a job, and keeping it for 40 years is rapidly becoming outdated. Opportunities for career or business growth are now more abundant than ever before in the history of humanity. Because of this, we must be aware of our needs, our talents, our desires both in the workplace and out if we want to embark on a path of growth, whichever that may be. Knowing what it is that you want will give you an edge over everyone else. You will give a sense of direction and purpose, while most will continue their living in reaction to whatever cards life deals them.

However, it doesn't stop there. Coaching yourself through self-questioning will help you, for instance, become a better decision maker. When practiced regularly, it will help you recognize the grey areas of your character and conduct let you know what you need to work on. When you have a better understanding of your desires, shortcomings, habits, and priorities, you will be empowered to initiate changes. The more aware you are of yourself, the better you'll understand your reasons behind your own decisions.

The Gift of Having a Purpose

There is a fine line between living and merely surviving. Having a definite set of goals that make you enthusiastically leap out of bed every morning; that, my friend, is living. When getting through the work week seems like a very difficult task, and you find solace on the promise of the weekend, then you are probably just trying to survive. Sit down. Think. Are you pleased with your life as it is? Is that really what you are going to do for the rest of your life? Successful people acquired success not because they had it all figured out. It's because they sat down and discovered their purpose. And once they identified it, they went in pursuit of it.

This is the gift of self-awareness- the ability to pursue something with abandonment because you know it's taking you where you really want to be, not because people around you dictate you to do so. Thus, self-awareness and life purpose go hand in hand.

Tips to Keep in Mind

I encourage you to complete this book and reflect on the things that matter most; to look inside yourself and be honest about the confusion you're going through without being embarrassed about it. Sometimes, in the process of self-discovery, we tend to judge ourselves in a punitive manner and are usually overly critical about our faults. This is not the correct mindset to approach the questions as they will only lead to a state of helplessness. Negativity is something we must avoid if we seek growth in any aspect of life.

Don't judge yourself too harshly. Instead, we invite you to take a more self-reflective approach and acknowledge the things that could have caused your shortcomings. Be nonjudgmental about rejections, accept the fact that everyone gets to experience failure, and prepare yourself to succeed in the next occasion. As Anthony Robbins would say, "See things as they are, but not worse than they are."

How to Use These Questions to Coach Others

When you think about leaders that have worked with you and impacted your life, what is it that you remember about them? Is it their performance during operations? Is it their perfect attendance? Or perhaps all the papers you were asked to submit? Not at all. What you remember is how they tried to connect with you – the genuineness and the ability to understand you on a deeper perspective as a person, not just an employee. That is how a leader makes an impact on his or her people's life and that is the idea that should be sub-communicated in the practice of coaching others.

Using the questioning method to coach other people requires two things: recognizing *what good leaders do* and learning *what the right questions* are. If you are able to fully understand these two, it will give you a clear framework for approaching those who need your advice.

What Good Leaders Do

What do good leaders do when coaching others? Though there's a lot taking place when a leader coaches someone, we can summarize them into three things:

1. First, a leader must be equipped with the ability to empathize with his people.
2. A good leader must lead their people into honest self-reflection.
3. A good leader must coach his people without destructive criticism or a personal agenda.

To put it simply, coaching is just having a sincere conversation with your people and asking them powerful questions to address, and hopefully resolve, their shortcomings. It doesn't have to be in form of a seminar or meeting, just an engaging one-on-one talk or any set-up that is most comfortable for the both of you. Just make sure that you keep those three points in mind when attempting to coach others with the questions you will encounter in this book.

Asking the Right Questions

To ask the right questions is to avoid putting the individual in an uncomfortable situation. Asking *why* can be crucial, as it can be judgmental or too confrontational, especially if not delivered carefully. Open-ended, on the other hand, can be more encouraging. If an employee makes a mistake, asking him "What was your intention with that?" sounds more empathetic than simply asking "Why did you do it?" The wrong questions may only stir up our negative emotions.

But aside from choosing the right questions and proper deliverance, the most important thing is to show that you are genuinely curious to hear their answers. Not because that's what you are supposed to do according to the rules, but because genuinely care for the other's wellbeing.

Tips to Keep in Mind

The act of asking instead of suggesting may be the foundation of this method, but its success does not entirely rely on the right questions. When approaching somebody for coaching, your main goal should be to evoke a sense of certainty and awareness in the other. Your willingness to listen to the answers and your ability to decipher the emotions encrypted in every word (as not everyone will be comfortable to open up immediately) and to adapt your approach accordingly will facilitate the coaching process.

EMPLOYEES: *On People and Professional Relationships*

"The road to success and the road to failure are almost exactly the same."

1.) How comfortable are you with your co-workers? Who do you usually hang out with during lunch breaks? Does being with these people (or person) contribute to your happiness in the workplace? And if so, in what way?

2.) List down 5 workmates whom you consider your closest friends at work. What do you do to please them (or to please a friend in general)? How important do you think interpersonal relationships are in the workplace?

"Success is not final; failure is not fatal: It is the courage to continue that counts."

3.) What other interests do you share with your co-workers that are not related to work? How did you discover these similarities? Given a chance, what activities would you like to do with your co-workers that may help you unwind and loosen up?

4.) Give at least 3 kinds of traits that you look for in an ideal teammate. How important are these traits to you? And how do you think these traits will affect your performance in general?

"Opportunities don't just happen; you create them."

5.) On a scale of 1 to 5, how comfortable are you in terms of opening up to your superior? Try to give at least 3 factors that make you feel either at ease or uneasy (depending on the rate you've given) around these people. Please elaborate on each.

6.) List down 5 behaviors that you think people might not like about you. Which one do you think could be the worst? How do you feel about these behaviors? Do you think it is something that you can actually work on?

"The most successful men in the end
are those whose success is the result of steady accretion."

7.) What forms of gesture or body language do you consider as signs that people do not like you? How do you feel about it? And how do you handle the thought that some people might not like you for what you are?

8.) List down or think of 3 misunderstanding incidents you've had with a co-worker in the past. Next, reflect on the biggest one. What did you do to resolve the issue? Were you happy or satisfied with the way you handled the situation?

"Nothing reinforces a professional relationship more than enjoying the success with someone."

9.) Think of any (small) misunderstanding or argument you once had with your superior. What had been the reason for this? How did you manage to explain yourself without escalating the tension? Were you satisfied with the way you handled the situation?

10.) Misunderstandings at the workplace are inevitable, but what exactly is your mindset towards this? How do you try to avoid miscommunication with your co-workers? And what is the importance of addressing work-related issues immediately?

EMPLOYEES: On Achievements and Failures

"I find that the harder I work, the more luck I seem to have."

11.) Recall at least 3 achievements you've reached in the past couple of years. Which among these do you consider the largest? How did you manage to achieve it? Were there any sacrifices that had to be done in order to obtain it?

12.) Give at least 3 "smaller" achievements you had this (or last) year. How did they help you come up with a fresher work perspective? How do small things actually contribute to a bigger success?

"There are two types of people who will tell you that you cannot make a difference in this world: those who are afraid to try and those who are afraid you will succeed."

13.) What do you do to celebrate achievements? And how do celebrations help you in terms of maintaining your enthusiasm towards your work?

14.) What piece of advice can you give someone who wanted to achieve something in his professional life, but is being discouraged by his failures in the past?

"Never give in except to convictions of honor and good sense."

15.) How does an achievement, no matter how small or big it is, change someone's perspective towards work? How did your own professional achievement change yours?

16.) What particular task do you feel you actually failed at? What do you think could be the reason for this? And given a chance, how would you handle the same task to get a better result?

"I owe my success to having listened respectfully to the very best advice, and then going away and doing the exact opposite."

17.) Think about the 3 most recent work-related failures you had. What did you learn from these events, personally and professionally? How do you think these experiences could help you become a better person?

18.) It is innate for us to celebrate achievements, but how do you usually handle failures? Do you think failures can be looked at in a positive way? And if so, what do you do in order to absorb it without being discouraged?

"If you are not willing to risk the usual, you will have to settle for the ordinary."

19.) How would you encourage someone to not lose hope after failing at something? Do you think relaying your personal story of failure may actually help encourage an individual to try again and start anew? If so, what would be your approach on this?

20.) On a scale of 1 to 5, how comfortable are you in terms of discussing a task you failed at with your superior? How do you think this kind of discussion may help you do better next time?

EMPLOYEES: On Short and Long-Term Goals

"If you really look closely, most overnight successes took a long time."

21.) List down at least 5 short-term, professional goals you wish to achieve this year. In how long (weeks or months) do you wish to achieve each goal? What course of action do you plan in order to accomplish them?

22.) List down at least 3 long-term, professional goals you wish to achieve in the coming years. In how many years do you wish to achieve each goal? What course of action do you plan in order to accomplish them?

"The successful warrior is the average man, with laser-like focus."

23.) What do you think is the importance of setting smaller goals before going for the bigger ones? When can you consider a goal as short-term? How about as long-term?

24.) How do you see yourself in about 5 years? What significant changes do you wish to acquire in your life, both personal and professional, by this time? Do you still see yourself in the same line of work, or perhaps get your feet wet on a different field?

"Character cannot be developed in ease and quiet. Only through experience of trial and suffering can the soul be strengthened, ambition inspired, and success achieved."

25.) How do goals affect our mindset towards work? Do you think setting a particular goal make us mentally stronger? If so, in what way?

EMPLOYEES: On Life Outside Work

"Fall seven times; stand up eight."

26.) What do you usually do to unwind? Do you think that social activities can actually affect an individual's professional performance? In what way do you think it contributes to your creativity at work?

27.) When you are neither working nor socializing, how do you usually relax at home? What does personal space mean to you? And how do you think having your personal space may contribute to your ability to work better?

"Our greatest weakness lies in giving up. The most certain way to success is always to try just one more time."

28.) Think of at least 5 nonwork-related topics you enjoy talking about with your family or friends. How do these things make you happy? How healthy do you think it is to wander your mind off the work-related stories and stuff?

29.) Most jobs can be sedentary. What do you do (or at least intend to do) in order to maintain your physical health during your days off? How do you think a good physical condition may help us accomplish a lot more at work?

"Travel and change of place impart new vigor to the mind."

30.) When you think of a vacation leave, what activities come to your mind? How often do you wish you could unwind?

EMPLOYEES: On Self-Improvement

"A successful man is one who can lay a firm foundation with the bricks that others throw at him."

31.) On a scale of 1 to 5, how happy are you right now in terms of career? Is there anything in particular that you wish to change about your work routine? How will this affect your performance and happiness in the workplace?

32.) List down 5 good skills (work-related) that are proven to help you with your daily work routine. Which among these do you consider the best? What new skills would you like to develop that may satisfy you professionally?

"The only place where success comes before work is in the dictionary."

33.) Think of the recent challenges you have encountered at work. How do you think challenges can be a good way to push someone to become more strong-willed? How do you usually handle challenges in your personal and professional life?

34.) What is the essence of having a particular role model to observe? Who do you look up to in terms of professional success? When do you think an individual should carry out changes to further improve himself?

"Be so busy improving yourself that you have no time to criticize others."

35.) Think of the challenges you've had recently. When was the last time you felt the need to change and improve yourself? What was the reason behind this? Whose advice do you seek in times like this?

EMPLOYEES: On Leadership

"Find somebody to be successful for. Raise their hopes. Think of their needs."

36.) What kind of work culture would you like to create, if given a chance? How do you think the culture in the workplace affects people's perspective towards work in general? What are the elements of a good working environment?

37.) What do you think could be the reasons for someone to lose his motivation to work? And if you are in the position to help, how would you bring out the best in that person and push him or her to grow professionally?

"It is better to fail in originality than to succeed in imitation."

38.) Aside from your individual ability, how can you be of help in terms of team performance? What traits do you think you possess that could help your team to excel? What is the essence of teamwork for you?

39.) When do you usually help a colleague? Is there a limit when it comes to helping someone with his tasks? What could be the downside of always lending your colleagues a hand, if you can think of any?

"Success usually comes to those who are too busy to be looking for it."

40.) What traits do you believe a good leader should possess? Give at least 3 and try to elaborate each. Now observe yourself for a while, what particular leadership trait do you possess and how can you make use of it?

EMPLOYEES: On Purpose and Self-Awareness

"Success seems to be connected with action. Successful people keep moving. Of course, they make mistakes, but they don't quit."

41.) List down 3 passions, or any sort of interest you love doing the most. How do these activities make you happy? Despite your busy schedule and responsibilities, how do you try to squeeze in a quick "me-time" to unwind and do these activities?

42.) In what circumstance do you get most excited or motivated? How often do you feel this way? More particularly, when was the last time you felt excited about something, and what was it? How do you think exciting activities can be beneficial for you as an individual?

"One can have no smaller or greater mastery
than mastery of oneself."

43.) When was the last time you felt most engaged in your work? What were you doing then? What are the elements of a fulfilling job, in your own opinion?

44.) List down at least 5 people that you look up to as professional individuals. What do these people have that made them good role models? How do you try to be a good example to others, just like these people?

"The people who succeed are irrationally passionate about something."

45.) In what way do you think your workmates would describe you? Are you worried that some of them may actually have something unpleasant to say about you? Or are you confident in your relationship with them? If so, why?

46.) Granted that you have enough time and money to do anything you want, what would you be doing at this moment? Who would you create experiences with?

"There is a powerful driving force inside every human being that, once unleashed, can make any vision, dream, or desire a reality."

47.) What was your first ideal job when you were younger? Did you really see yourself pursuing this career? How different is your first ideal job to the job that you have right now? What caused your change of mind?

48.) What is your own, personal definition of being successful? And at what age do you wish to become totally successful, both personally and professionally?

"Don't be afraid to give up the good to go for the great."

49.) If you were to leave your company tomorrow, what legacy would you leave behind? How would people remember you? What reputation have you built for yourself?

50.) On a scale of 1 to 5, how balanced do you think your work-life routine is? What do you think could be the reason for this? If your answer is 2 or below, how do you plan to change your routine in order to rebalance everything?

EMPLOYEES: On (Separating) Personal and Work-Related Issues

"Success is how high you bounce when you hit bottom."

51.) Do you have any worries at home or at work that you think should be given attention right now? How do you usually to fix issues without affecting the quality of your work or personal life? And aside from professionalism, why is it important to separate personal issues from work-related ones?

52.) Problems at home are inevitable, but how do you get to face your professional responsibilities despite carrying the emotional burden? When is the right time for someone to finally take a vacation leave and try to loosen up?

Try not to become a man of success. Rather become a man of value."

53.) Do you know anyone at work who may be emotionally burdened? If so, what can you do to try to ease this person's burden?

54.) What are the signs that a person is actually mixing up his personal issues with work-related ones? How can it affect this person and other people who are directly working with him?

"Success is walking from failure to failure with no loss of enthusiasm."

55.) What kind of support structure do you think emotionally burdened employees should have? How can a support group help in terms of lightening up this person's mindset towards everything?

EMPLOYEES: *Random IF Questions*

"The master has failed more times than the beginner has even tried."

56.) If you were to teach someone how to lighten up, be happier, be more enthusiastic – or basically anything positive, what exactly would you tell this person? What kind of approach would you use in order to show how to be optimistic?

57.) If your superior were to assign you to organize a recreational team excursion, how exactly would you plan it? Give at least 5 fun activities you'd love to include and please elaborate on each.

"Celebrate your successes. Find some humor in your failures."

58.) If you were not in the current industry you're in, what kind of job do you think you'd be doing? How different would things have turned out if you landed on a totally different line of work?

59.) If you could go back in time, what particular regretful event would you try to change? What is your reason for choosing this, and how would it change the current situation you're in?

"Outstanding people have one thing in common: An absolute sense of mission."

60.) If you could be anyone influential for 24 hours, who would you choose to be? How would you make use of your time limit in making significant changes in people's lives (perhaps including yours)?

EMPLOYEES: On Financial Matters

"Many of life's failures are people who did not realize how close they were to success when they gave up."

61.) At what age do you wish to be financially stable? What do you think are the common reasons that hold people back from becoming financially secure?

62.) What are the things you need to consider with respect to saving money? Do you have financial priorities? What are they? How can you improve them? How can you make better use of your money to achieve financial stability?

"Put your heart, mind, and soul into even your smallest acts. This is the secret of success."

63.) Do you think you are well-compensated for the amount of work and stress that you acquire on a daily basis? Salary is a common driving factor to keep an employee motivated, but when do you think salary alone isn't enough to continue working?

64.) What are the things that you prioritize when it comes to spending your hard-earned money? Are you usually willing to spend on your relaxation and leisure? If so, what could be the benefits of allotting a budget for self-pleasure?

"Success consists of going from failure to failure
without loss of enthusiasm."

65.) Is it really practical to accept a high-paying job with a really stressful nature? If you were given this offer, what factors would you consider before accepting or turning it down?

EMPLOYEES: *On Time Management*

"The path to success is to take massive, determined action."

66.) How do you usually start your day, from the moment you leave your bed up until you reach the workplace? What activities take up most of your time every day?

67.) How do you budget your time in order to organize your daily tasks? What activities do you usually put on top of your priorities? Do you get to finish most of them, or do you often run out of time before getting things done?

"Successful people do what unsuccessful people are not willing to do. Don't wish it were easier; wish you were better."

68.) How can proper time management affect an employee's performance? What do you think are the usual factors that hinder an individual from managing his time well? Can you recall an incident wherein improper time-handling affects your performance so bad?

69.) What are the things you often prioritize during the work week and the things you prioritize during your days off? Do you think that taking home some work is reasonable?

"Only those who dare to fail greatly can ever achieve greatly."

70.) What is an ideal time management plan for you? Try to create a short one and explain in details. Then answer these two questions: In what way do you think this plan is ideal? What is stopping you from actually putting this ideal plan into action?

71.) Think of an activity that you have put off doing for a long time. It could be a particular task at work, a hobby, or just anything that you wish to do, but still haven't. What's stopping you from actually doing it?

"Always bear in mind that your own resolution to succeed is more important than any other one thing."

72.) Do you write a to-do list? Do you think it is an effective way to keep track of your supposed activities for the day?

73.) Recall the last time you procrastinated. What was the reason for this delay and how did this affect you (personally or professionally)? Is it an isolated case, or are you really having a hard time following schedules? Please elaborate.

"Do you want to know who you are? Don' ask. Act! Action will delineate and define you."

74.) At the end of each day, are you usually satisfied with the number of things that you get done? How often do you feel productive? And what exactly do you feel about unfinished chores or tasks?

75.) Time management is a useful skill in any workplace, but how can it help you in terms of your personal life? Do you think time management is still necessary at home? How can you put this into practice?

EMPLOYEES: On Getting Unstuck

"Before anything else, preparation is the key to success."

76.) Describe your current work-life situation. How's that working for you so far? How exactly does the thought of getting up for work make you feel?

77.) On your days off, do you look forward or at least intend to do fun things to break your routine? Or were you simply hoping to catch up on your sleep? Is there anything in particular that makes you feel excited about going to work?

"The secret of success is to do the common things uncommonly well"

78.) Some people are afraid of changes; afraid of facing new challenges outside their comfort zone. How about you? Can you think of at least 3 things that you are actually afraid of? – Things that are probably getting in the way of your dreams, or living the life that you want?

79.) What elements in your life are you willing and ready to change? And what are those that you are not ready for at this point? What are the things that you usually consider before acknowledging that you are not ready for something yet?

"The ones who are crazy enough to think they can change the world,
are the ones that do."

80.) With all honesty, what bad habits do you need to stop doing? What makes it difficult to change or stop in the first place?

EMPLOYEES: On Constant Learning

"If you are working on something exciting that you really care about, you don't have to be pushed. The vision pulls you."

81.) Considering all the things you have gone through in the past 5 years, what life lessons have you learned? Among these lessons, what do you think was the biggest? How did it affect your life?

82.) What was the most significant wisdom you have acquired in your life? Did someone impose this on you, or did you acquire it from your own experience? Do you believe you're already wise enough to get you through hardships?

"Success is liking yourself, liking what you do,
and liking how you do it."

83.) How do you take criticism? What, for you, is the difference between constructive and offensive criticism, and how do you recognize them?

84.) When someone criticizes you, does it affect your confidence or lessen your motivation, in any way? Who do you normally talk to when you want to confide about not being confident on something?

"Measure your success according to fun and creativity."

85.) If you can share any of your experience and knowledge to the younger ones, what particular event in your life would you share? How would you relate this story to your audience in order to inspire them?

"Do not watch the clock; do what it does. Keep going."

86.) How different is your mindset this day from your mindset 5 years ago? What particularly has changed? And how did you cope with these changes? Do you believe you are in a better disposition this time?

87.) When you reach your senior stage in life, how would you like to look back? What exactly are the things you'd like to remember? And what sense of fulfillment do you wish to acquire by this age?

"When your desires are strong enough, you will appear to possess superhuman powers to achieve them."

88.) What life lesson do you wish you have known earlier? Granting that it's possible, what particular event in your life would you like to do over again? And what would you do differently?

89.) What kind of wisdom or lesson do you wish you could impart to people? In what way do you want to help those who are undecided about their career or personal life?

"Do one thing every day that scares you."

90.) Do you believe that there's always an opportunity to learn in every situation? How do you seek new knowledge or wisdom to further improve yourself?

EMPLOYEES: *Journal Prompts*

"The ladder of success is never crowded at the top."

In this part, we will complete the prompts provided below. It could be just a few sentences or an entire paragraph depending on how much you want to share. Nevertheless, I encourage you to go into details. Use no filter.

91.) I may not be perfect, but I always try to be the best version of myself by…

92.) I understand and comply with my obligations as a responsible adult, but I like to keep in touch with my inner child by …

"All progress takes place outside the comfort zone."

93.) I am happy being around those I love, like…

94.) I believe it is important to take a break and make time for my passion which is…

"Don't let the fear of losing be greater than the excitement of winning."

95.) Failure is an important part of an individual's career and personal growth because...

96.) Finding and working towards our purpose in life is something we should never get tired of doing because…

"The only limit to our realization of tomorrow will be our doubts of today."

97.) We should have a good understanding of our financial health because...

98.) I respect people who...

"The way to get started is to quit talking and begin doing."

99.) Constantly growing and exceeding yourself despite problems and personal issues is important because...

100.) I can describe my life as...

LEADERS AND BUSINESS OWNERS: On People and Professional Relationships

"Success is a science; if you have the conditions, you get the result."

1.) How strict or easy-going are you with your employees? Do you try to interact with them when your schedule permits? Does being with your people contribute to your overall happiness in the workplace? Please explain.

2.) List down 5 employees or co-leaders whom you consider closest to you. How is your relationship with them? How can you improve it? How should an individual with a leadership role grow interpersonal relationships?

"The success of any great moral enterprise
does not depend upon numbers."

3.) What other interests do you share with your people that are not related to work? To put more simply, how do you get to know your people when you are outside your work/professional space? What would you recommend your people to do in order to unwind and loosen up?

4.) Give at least 3 kinds of traits that you look for in an ideal employee. How important are these traits to you? And how do you think these traits will affect the business in general?

"The ability to convert ideas to things
is the secret of outward success."

5.) Personal problems may affect an individual's performance at work. On a scale of 1 to 5, how open are you in terms of listening to your employee's personal issues? As their superior, what can you do to help them feel better about themselves?

6.) List down 3 major behaviors that you think people might not like about you. What factors do you think contribute to these behaviors? And as a leader yourself, how do you feel about these behavioral issues? Do you think it is something that you can actually work on?

*"I measure success in terms of the contributions an individual
makes to her fellow human beings."*

7.) What forms of body language do you consider as strong signs that people may not be happy about their job? If you see one of your workers showing these signs, what steps are you going to take?

8.) List down 3 misunderstanding incidents among your workers. As their superior, what did you do (or do you have to do) to help them resolve their issues? In events like this, do you think leaders should really step in? Please elaborate.

"There are no secrets to success. It is the result of preparation, hard work, and learning from failure."

9.) Think of any misunderstanding or argument you had with an employee. What was the reason for it? How did you manage to fix the issue without escalating the tension? Do you think you handled the situation fairly?

10.) Misunderstandings at the workplace are inevitable. As someone in a leadership role, what exactly is your mindset towards this? What can you advise your people in order to avoid miscommunication with their fellow workers?

LEADERS AND BUSINESS OWNERS: *On Achievements and Failures*

"Be a student as long as you still have something to learn,
and this will mean all your life."

11.) Reminisce at least 3 achievements you have acquired as a leader in the past couple of years. Which among these do you consider the biggest? Can you try to look back at some of the things you had to sacrifice or focus on in order to achieve them?

12.) How do you recognize an employee's small yet significant achievement? What do you do to help them come up with a fresher work perspective? How do you think small things actually contribute to a business' success?

"I honestly think it is better to be a failure at something you love than to be a success at something you hate."

13.) How do you celebrate your team's achievement? How can you help the workers in maintaining their enthusiasm towards work? And what exactly is the role of enthusiasm in team productivity?

14.) How can you lift someone's spirit when he is being discouraged by his past failures? What piece of advice are you going to give this person in order to get him back on track?

"Never give up on what you really want to do. The person with big dreams is more powerful than one with all the facts."

15.) How did your past achievements change your perspective towards work? Was there ever a time that you felt like giving up? Did you ever look up at a certain leader before you became a leader yourself?

16.) How do you feel when a worker fails to deliver quality work? Do you normally get angry, or do you give this person a chance to explain his reason? How do you think leaders should handle disappointments caused by non-performing employees?

*"Small daily improvements over time lead
to stunning results."*

17.) Think about the biggest failure you had as a business person or a leader. What did you learn from this event, and how did this failure make you the person that you are today?

18.) How do you teach your people to take failures positively, considering that they look up to you during the tough times?

"Success seems to be connected with action. Successful people keep moving. They make mistakes, but they don't quit."

19.) Do you think that, as a leader, it is okay to share your own success story (success in terms of being promoted or chosen to be a leader) to those who are starting to lose hope? What is your take on this? Please elaborate.

20.) Some employees needed more time before he is able to adapt to his work environment. This sometimes leads to bad performance or quality of work. How do you think a one-on-one talk with this employee may help him do better next time?

LEADERS AND BUSINESS OWNERS: *Starting a Business*

"No one is unsmart. Everyone's a genius at something.
Our job is to find it. And then encourage it."

21.) What was your main reason for creating a team or business? Can you list down the primary factors that influenced your decision?

22.) Initially, when you first started your business, what product or service did you want to offer? Is the product or service you currently offer different from your original idea? How many times did you change your mind before you actually came up with the final one?

*"Some people dream of success, while other people get up
every morning and make it happen."*

23.) What is the added value that accompanies the sale of your products
or services? What change or impact in the lives of others are you trying
to pursue? Are you passionate about this cause?

24.) Were you ready to commit yourself – along with your time and
attention – in order to be successful in the field that you have chosen?
What were the first major setbacks and difficulties you encountered?

*"The successful man will profit from his mistakes
and try again in a different way."*

25.) How did your life change as a whole? Did you have to give up some of your hobbies or leisure activities? Did you discover a new sense of strength within you, or perhaps new weaknesses? Please elaborate.

26.) Handling a business could be very exhausting, and it is imperative that you be in a good mental, physical and emotional condition in order to run it well. How was your overall health status when you started working on your business? Has it improved? If not, what can you do to make sure you're operating at 100%?

"Twenty years from now you will be more disappointed by the things that you didn't do than by the ones you did do. So throw off the bowlines. Sail away from the safe harbor. Catch the trade winds in your sails. Explore. Dream. Discover."

27.) Getting your feet wet on a business venture requires being financially ready for the expenses that are about to come. How were you able to accomplish the financial requirements involving the business? Do you think seeking professional financial advice is really needed? What are your thoughts on this?

28.) Do you believe you possess all the necessary skills to control the operations on a daily basis? Or did you ask someone to help you out with it?

*"As a general rule, the most successful man in life
is the man who has the best information."*

29.) Do you consider yourself tech-savvy? Do you think you have an up-to-date knowledge of tools and applications that could make business run smoothly? If not, how do you plan to adapt to this?

30.) Do you think your academic background was enough to sustain your long-term business goals? Are you willing to get certifications or take short courses to widen your knowledge in your field of expertise? Why or why not?

"I learned to always take on things I'd never done before.
Growth and comfort do not coexist."

31.) Despite many other similar businesses around the country, what do you think makes your business unique? What advantages do you have that may actually beat your competitors?

32.) Running a business will be impossible without your key players. How did you choose your management team? The operations employees? How crucial is it for startups to hire the right people, and most importantly, how can hiring the wrong ones affect your operations as a whole?

"I cannot give you the formula for success, but I can give you the formula for failure –
It is: Try to please everybody."

33.) What type of market do you target? And how, in the first place, are you planning to sell your products or services to this particular market?

34.) What are the elements of a successful business? How do we identify whether or not the business has the potential to be sustainable? And if worst comes to worst, when do we say that it is more practical to stop than acquire more financial damage?

"Success is not the key to happiness. Happiness is the key to success.
If you love what you are doing, you will be successful."

35.) How big, really, is the market you are trying to enter? How important is it to estimate the potential profit before actually getting yourself in?

LEADERS AND BUSINESS OWNERS: Running the Business

"Life shrinks or expands in proportion to one's courage."

36.) Write about your typical at work. Who help you run the business, and how are responsibilities usually shared?

37.) How do you address work-related issues? And as a leader, entrepreneur, or business owner, how crucial is it to fix misunderstandings immediately?

"You learn more from failure than from success.
Don't let it stop you. Failure builds character."

38.) Do you regret having or not having done something that relates to your business? Share how you would have done things differently if given the chance.

39.) Share with us one successful customer service story to inspire people to always give their best. Focus on the impact you have left into this customer's life.

"Integrity is more valuable than income. Honor is richer than fame. Self-Worth is wealthier than net worth."

40.) Explain briefly how intricate it was to establish your own management team. Mention the factors that you had to consider.

41.) What are the things that have contributed to your success as a leader or entrepreneur? Did you ever encounter things that got in the way?

*"Most of the successful people I've known are the ones
who do more listening than talking."*

42.) How do you define being fair? How is fairness an essential part of anyone's success?

43.) How did your product or service evolve in the past few years? How did you and your partners – along with your workers – adjust to this evolution?

"Success comes from knowing that you did your best
to become the best that you are capable of becoming."

44.) Discuss one mistake that (almost) took its toll on the business, what particular decisions led to it?

45.) Behind every successful leader, owners or entrepreneur is a good mentor. Discuss the knowledge and wisdom you acquired from this person. How did you apply it to the business?

"Champions keep on playing until they get it right."

46.) What do you think is the biggest challenge in the industry you are in? How does it affect the employees, business owners, and entrepreneur in general? State your opinion.

47.) How do you think leaders and business owners should take advantage of technology in running a business?

"Success is not the key to happiness. Happiness is the key to success. If you love what you are doing, you will be successful."

48.) Is it really helpful to follow prominent businessmen's profile (Twitter, Facebook, etc) online? How can these people influence our perspective towards the business? And if so, who do you think we should actually follow? Please elaborate.

49.) When creating marketing strategies, who do you consult first before coming up with a major decision? What makes brainstorming and extensive research significant steps in creating business tactics?

"There is no scientific answer for success. You can't define it. You've simply got to live it and do it."

50.) Aside from the academic background, what personality traits do you strictly look for in an employee when you're hiring people? In what way are these traits important in the business?

51.) Tell us the story behind your brand creation. Reminisce the time when you were just considering putting together a team or business. What were the constraints you encountered? And what made you finally decide to go for it? How about the meaning of your brand name or logo?

"The key to success is to keep growing in all areas of life
– mental, emotional, spiritual, as well as physical."

52.) What are the elements of a successful product launching? List down at least 3 major steps that have to be taken into consideration.

53.) What traits should a strong-willed leader, business owner or entrepreneur have? How are these traits going to help you in the industry you're in?

"You've got to get up every morning with determination if you're going to go to bed with satisfaction."

54.) How is attending an industry-related seminar or conference going to be helpful for a business? Please look back at one particular event you attended in the past; what takeaways or realization did you bring with you upon leaving?

55.) What modern tools or form of social media can you use to let people constantly hear and read about your brand? What is your personal take on online brand advertising?

*"Success in any endeavor depends on the degree
to which it is an expression of your true self."*

56.) Share at least one thing about the industry you are in. It doesn't have to be a major company secret – just something that people outside the industry probably do not know about. What makes it interesting?

57.) When interviewing a potential employee: Give at least 3 major questions that you should ask your applicant – something not written in the resume. How important is it to actually ask these questions?

"I'd rather attempt to do something great and fail
than to attempt to do nothing and succeed."

58.) Reflection: Are you comfortable with the level at which business is operating at this moment? Do you wish to stay at this level, or do you plan on pursuing growth aggressively? How are your actions reflecting your goals?

59.) What made you decide to venture into the industry you are in? What makes it worth it, in comparison to others? And what makes it suitable for your personality and expertise?

"Success isn't just about what you accomplish in your life;
It's about what you inspire others to do."

60.) Are there any business sayings or quotes that you have tried to reflect on? How do they make you feel about your business venture?

61.) What do you think is the most challenging thing about your brand or industry? And how do you get to handle the stress that comes with it?

"Many of life's failures are people who did not realize
how close they were to success when they gave up."

62.) How do you picture your brand in about 5 years? Try to imagine and put into words.

63.) If you can speak directly to your younger self, what particular wisdom are you going to share that would help him get through the trials and come up even stronger in the present time?

"Don't be distracted by criticism.
Remember--the only taste of success some people get is to take a bite out of
you."

64.) Let's say you are not in your current industry, what are you doing instead? Was your current job even your first choice? Please elaborate.
65.) Should we ever be satisfied with the current status of our business or brand? What is the importance of constantly wanting to improve it?

LEADERS AND BUSINESS OWNERS: *Reflections*

"Good things happen to those who hustle."

I want you to answer this in a more detailed and personal way. This may work as a diary; no judgment, no particular answer – just you being honest with yourself.

66.) What is your WHY for your business? What made it worth the risk?

67.) Success, no matter how much we prepare for the trials, is never guaranteed. How do you prepare yourself for possible failures?

"The man who has confidence in himself
gains the confidence of others."

68.) Your life doesn't just revolve around the business; you have other responsibilities, too. How can you focus on one thing without compromising the other?

69.) A business startup is more like a trial-and-error. You're not sure about the outcome, but you're learning ways on how to strengthen your foundation. What is your image of a strong business foundation?

"Arriving at one goal is the starting point to another."

70.) Your target market or ideal customer has to have a clear understanding of the products or services you offer. How did you come up with your product's concept?

71.) You probably have other options, like working for a big company, becoming a freelancer, etc. But why did you choose to have a business in the first place?

*"Success is achieved and maintained by those
who try and keep trying."*

72.) An establishment's validity is important. How did you work on the legal requirements of your business?

73.) Having a business will make your schedule all the more hectic. Do you believe that having a business partner would make things easier, or you prefer being on your own?

"If we did all the things we are capable of,
we would literally astound ourselves."

74.) In order to start a business, one must have enough capital to take care of all the expenses that come with it. Should you, or other aspiring business people, consider applying for a loan to get started?

75.) It is not always going to be smooth-sailing. We know that problems are going to come up one way or another. Where or who can you turn to for help?

"You can teach a student a lesson for a day; but if you can teach him to learn by creating curiosity, he will continue the learning process as long as he lives."

76.) It is not every time that you are going to receive compliments from other business people. How do you take criticisms?

77.) Running a business requires speaking to a lot of people, and probably attending different events in hopes of expanding your network. How open and confident are you in terms of meeting new people?

"However difficult life may seem, there is always something you can do and succeed."

78.) Any brand needs exposure and plugging. What is your approach to business advertising?

79.) How did you consider the location of your business? Is it something that you can set up at home for the meantime, or does renting a small business space sound more professional?

"There are no secrets to success.
It is the result of preparation, hard work, and learning from failure."

80.) Every business starts off small. But how big is an ideal startup for you, and how big do you wish it turns out in the future?

81.) We all want to have a sense of freedom in terms of handling our schedule and not having to follow anyone's instructions. What do you like most about being self-employed?

*"A good plan violently executed now is better than
a perfect plan executed next week."*

82.) Say, the business shows constant improvement, when do you think is the right time to expand your number of employees?

83.) You can't expect people to purchase your service or product if you cannot even talk about it in detail. How strong is your product knowledge and how can you differentiate it from others?

"Success seems to be connected with action. Successful people keep moving. They make mistakes, but they don't quit"

84.) Your family is your most genuine support group. But is it okay to hire a family member?

85.) Proper behavior in the workplace contributes a lot to its success. How do you personally discipline (or what is your personal approach on) unethical behavior?

"Success is not built on success. It's built on failure. It's built on frustration. Sometimes it's built on catastrophe."

86.) In a world where promotions and advertisements are better done online, how d personal recommendation and word-of-mouth work for you?

87.) With proper training and genuine care, there will always be good employees that will serve as assets to the business. How should we take care of talented employees?

"Perfection is not attainable, but if we chase perfection
we can catch excellence."

88.) Customer satisfaction, at times, can be elusive. How do you handle irate customers? How do you work on their complaints?

89.) Up to what extent are you willing to adjust in order to satisfy a regular customer?

"You have to believe that you are the one who creates your success;
that you are the one who creates your mediocrity,
and that you are the one creating your struggle around money and success."

90.) For startups, when is it safe to finally expand the business (Expand, like probably hire more people, open a second branch, etc)?

91.) As a self-employed individual, up to what extent are you will be hands-on just to deliver customer satisfaction?

"The most successful people are mavericks who aren't afraid to ask why, especially when everyone thinks it's obvious."

92.) What is your biggest fear about the business?

93.) Coming up with the business' overall concept requires extensive research. Do we really need to come up with a hundred percent original idea, or is it okay to get inspiration from other business establishments?

"Keep on going, and the chances are that you will stumble on something,
perhaps when you are least expecting it.
I never heard of anyone ever stumbling on something sitting down."

94.) What kind of lifestyle do you have at the moment? Does your business support or complement the lifestyle that you really want?

95.) Is your business something you'd still have the enthusiasm to run 10 to 15 years from now? Please do elaborate.

"I never did anything worth doing by accident, nor did any of my inventions come indirectly through accident, except the phonograph. No, when I have fully decided that a result is worth getting, I go about it, and make trial after trial, until it comes."

96.) Can your business operate without your direct supervision? Please set a sample scenario.

97.) What is one thing that you will NEVER give up for business?

*"You know you are on the road to success if you would do your job,
and not be paid for it."*

98.) At the end of the day, what three major things do you wish to learn from all the stress of running a business?

99.) Do you see yourself expanding the business through franchising and/or branches? Picture it out, then try to put your imagination into words.

"You know you are on the road to success if you would do your job, and not be paid for it."

100.) Is it worth it for you?

Conclusion

I was recently in Quito, Ecuador in a massive convention for entrepreneurs. It had been 2 days already and I could feel my body using its last bits of energy. Suddenly I heard one of the speakers conclude his talk with the following:

"So, my friends, you have to learn to ask the right questions. Questions are very powerful tools for creating change. Ask yourself better questions and your life will improve. Ask others better questions and their life will improve. Always remember- questions are the vehicle of the mind. Thank you."

And so, came the inspiration to continue thinking up books that will help my readers question and assess different areas of their lives. Your career or business life is of extreme important as it affects directly other areas of your life. Unless we are conscious of the decisions we make day by day in respect of where we're taking our lives, we will continue living this area of our life in autopilot. Being conscious of our current state is the first step for change. Perhaps the second is asking ourselves better questions. I hope this book has helped you realize things about yourself in this area of your life. If you enjoyed it, we'd appreciate an honest review on Amazon.

Thank you,

Gerald